An Introduction to Econometric Forecasting and Forecasting Models

The Wharton Econometric Studies Series

Wharton Econometric Forecasting Associates and
Economics Research Unit
The University of Pennsylvania
F. Gerard Adams and Lawrence R. Klein, Coordinators

Stabilizing World Commodity Markets
    Edited by F. Gerard Adams and Sonia A. Klein
Econometric Modeling of World Commodity Policy
    Edited by F. Gerard Adams and Jere Behrman
An Introduction to Econometric Forecasting and Forecasting Models
    Lawrence R. Klein and Richard M. Young

The following is a partial list of the publications planned for the future.

Econometric Models for Latin America
Economic Policy for World Commodity Markets
Industrial Econometrics: Models of Industries and Sectors
Policy Simulation with the Wharton Quarterly Econometric Model
Regional Econometric Model Building
The Wharton Long-Term Model
The Wharton Quarterly Econometric Model, Mark V:
    Specification and Performance

An Introduction to Econometric Forecasting and Forecasting Models

Lawrence R. Klein
University of Pennsylvania

Richard M. Young
Wharton Econometric Forecasting
Associates, Inc.

LexingtonBooks
D.C. Heath and Company
Lexington, Massachusetts
Toronto

Library of Congress Cataloging in Publication Data

Klein, Lawrence Robert.
  An introduction to econometric forecasting and
forecasting models.

  (Wharton econometric studies series)
  1. Econometrics. 2. Economic forecasting—Mathemetical
models. I. Young, Richard M., joint author. II. Title.
HB141.K53   330'.01'82   79-1542
ISBN 0-669-02896-7

Published simultaneously in Canada

Printed in the United States of America

International Standard Book Number: 0-669-02896-7

Library of Congress Catalog Card Number: 79-1542

Contents

List of Figures

List of Tables

Preface

"Nobody believes that he can become a chemist by attending lectures and reading textbooks and journal articles. He should also devote time and energy to the real work in a laboratory."[a] It is difficult for us to choose better words to introduce this work than those Henri Theil used to introduce his textbook on econometrics. In a very real sense the laboratory work for this book has been the sixteen years of continuous forecasting and modeling experience of the Wharton forecasting group. Perhaps the most tangible evidence of the worth of that laboratory is the number of students and colleagues who have passed through it and now are actively engaged in econometric modeling and forecasting work throughout the world. The techniques described in this book were not the work of a single individual or group. The current state of development and continuing evolution of these techniques owe much to those who have worked with us in the past and continue to work with us. The material presented here is an attempt to distill that wealth of accumulated experience and make it available to students, economists, and practitioners of forecasting.

Where possible we have attempted to present material in a nontechnical fashion, while augmenting technical points or issues with illustrations or references. The field of econometric forecasting, however, is firmly rooted in the technical results of statistics and econometrics, and technical issues are occasionally unavoidable.

With some lecture background, chapters 1, 2, 4, and 5 should be accessible and useful to technically oriented students, extending from first- or second-year undergraduates to first-year graduate students. We hope and believe that the material will also be useful to users of econometric forecasts throughout the business and government sector.

Chapter 3 and appendix 4A are more technically oriented than the remainder of the book and are intended for the actual practitioner of modeling and forecasting. We hope that you will avoid many of the perils and pitfalls awaiting the unwary.

---

[a]Henri Theil, *Principles of Econometrics* (New York: Wiley, 1971), p. v.

An Introduction to Econometric Forecasting and Forecasting Models

1

The Model Approach To Economic Forecasting

There is no doubt that modeling is here to stay. During the period since 1960, models have grown from the arcane devices of a coterie of academics to become a major tool of analysis for both public- and private-sector decisions. They are used for studying the probable response of the economy to changes in federal government policy ranging from major tax and expenditure initiatives to farm price supports, minimum wage changes, grants-in-aid programs, and a wide variety of other topics. Business use includes modeling and projecting sales response to price decisions, projecting raw materials prices and wage levels, and capital budgeting problems. In virtually every field of economic analysis where decisions must be based on the uncertain future, models have appeared as a means of generating information for the decision process, either as the major vehicle for analysis or as an adjunct to other analytic and forecasting tools.

Modeling has been a tool in a wide variety of areas including virtually the entire range of physical and social sciences for some time. As a generic term, we might regard any attempt to reduce the description of phenomena to a set of stylized relationships which approximate the observed facts as a *modeling effort.* From this broad point of view, a wide range of human inquiries can be viewed as attempts to construct models. The types of models with which economists are concerned, however, can generally be characterized as being capable of mathematical representation. Moreover, for an econometrician, these models are stochastic and subject to empirical refutation. In their largest and most complex state, they are simultaneous, dynamic, nonlinear, and involve thousands of relationships. They can involve the expenditure of millions of dollars for their creation and hundreds of thousands of dollars for upkeep and maintenance. What advantages do these models offer that has propelled their use into so many areas and has justified the expenditures associated with them?

Why a Model Approach?

Economic models of the economy as a whole came into use during the 1930s and became particularly helpful in explaining the theory of output/employment determination expounded by J.M. Keynes. From theoretical models of Keynesian economics and independent attempts to construct dynamic models of the economic trade cycle, there was a natural progression into statistically estimated models for purposes of analyzing conditions in the real world.[1]

In economic theory, particularly macroeconomic theory and business cycle theory, compact, abstract models became the rule of the day. They reached a peak of usefulness in laying out the bare bones of the otherwise difficult to understand Keynesian system. They were small models that lent themselves readily to graphical display. The most elegant and compact one is Hicks's *IS–LM* curve, represented by

$$S(r,Y) = I(r,Y) \quad \text{savings/investment equation}$$

$$M = L(r,Y) \quad \text{liquidity preference equation}$$

where r = the interest rate

                         Y = income

These are two *implicit* functions in r and Y. The IS curve will generally be negatively sloped, while the *LM* curve will be positively sloped. With some stretch of the imagination, the present-day large-scale empirical models can be described as extensions of the *IS–LM* relationship.[2]

The two-dimensional graph of the *IS–LM* system has great pedagogical value in conveying understanding of macroeconomic principles (see figure 1–1).

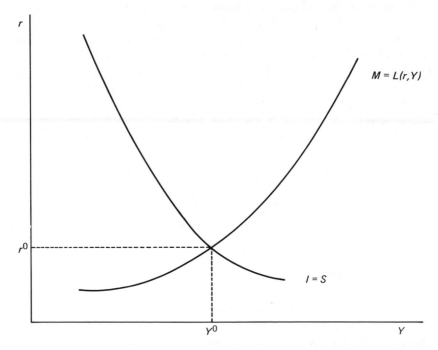

Figure 1-1. Graph of *IS–LM* Curves.

It is not, however, the model approach that is used in present-day forecasting, although it is the precursor of the large-scale forecasting model and contains the core of the system, capable of being derived on deeper analysis. In real-life situations today, it is necessary to try to take account of numerous matters of detail and a high degree of disaggregation. We must consider not only total investment as it is used on an aggregative plane in the I part of the IS relation, but at a minimum, we must also pay attention to inventory investment, business fixed investment, and residential investment, not to mention subcategories of each of these. Similarly, types of savings or their counterparts, types of consumption, must be given separate treatment. This is precisely what is done in the large forecasting models, together with added relationships on production, price formation, wage formation, and other variables.

Time-Series Analysis and Forecasting

Economic forecasting was a challenging practice before the advent of models. The standard practice was time-series analysis, that is to say, many individual time series were separately analyzed in terms of their own histories in order to project their futures. Historical series of steel production, wheat price, bond yields, building construction, stocks of coal, and hundreds of other variables were statistically processed, one by one, to gain insight into systematic patterns of behavior. A typical economic series, the time curve of U.S. industrial production, by quarters, appears in figure 1-2.

It can be seen immediately that this time curve has many characteristics:

1. It generally grows over long periods of two to three decades (trend component).
2. It has some marked upswings and downswings with a modicum of regularity (cyclical component).
3. It has jagged erratic aspects, some of which can be identified with major events—Korean war, Vietnam war, Suez Canal closing, oil embargo, etc. (random component).

One characteristic has already been extracted from this series, namely, its seasonal component which varies fairly regularly every year with summer, fall, winter, spring. The plotted series is *seasonally adjusted.*

The pure time-series analyst might pose the following interesting question: How do we look at the past and present of this series in order to arrive at a judgment about its future? Will the trend continue? Will the cycles repeat their course with some regularity? The average pattern of historic characteristics on trend development and periodicity, assuming neutral effects of random disturbances, constitute a framework for prediction or forecasting.

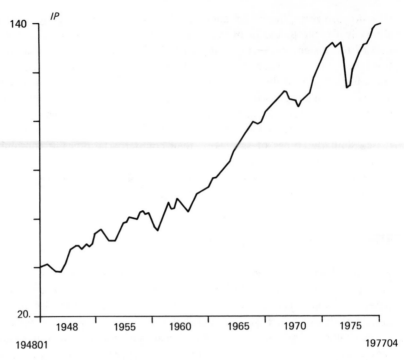

Figure 1-2. Federal Reserve Board Industrial Production Index, (1967 = 100.0).

There is no necessity to confine the analysis to the history of one series at a time. A standard way of looking at economic time series is to subdivide them into leaders, coinciders, and laggards as in figure 1-3, on the presumption that after the leaders have given some advance signal, the coinciders and laggards will follow in regular order. The leaders consist of such series as orders for durable goods, stock market price, length of working week, layoff rate, new business formation, new building permits, and similar advance indicators.

There are basically two ways of dealing with pure time-series analysis in economic forecasting. One method combines chart reading with judgment and various "nonparametric" statistics. The latter are measures of the standing of series in various phases of the cycle, the percent leading, the percent rising or falling, and timing characteristics. This approach is loose, flexible, and partly qualitative, partly quantitative. It does not depend strictly on a mathematical structure and relationship with identifiable parameters. The other method is more formal. It may relate present standing of a series to its past history by a

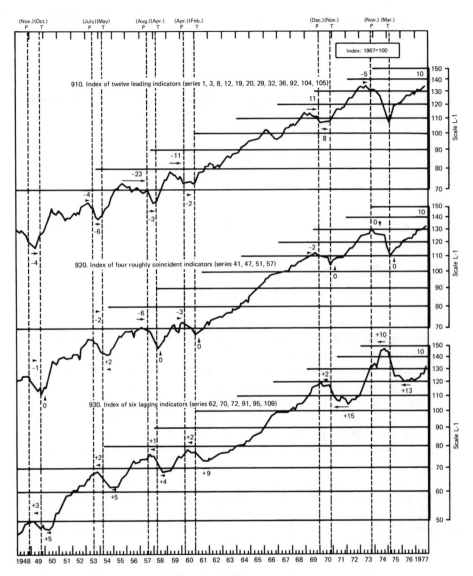

Source: *Business Conditions Digest.* (Washington, D.C.: U.S. Dept. of Commerce).

Figure 1-3. Cyclical Indicators, Composite Indexes and Their Components.

lag-correlation equation. Let y_t be industrial production at time t; then the lag correlation equation would be

$$y_t = \alpha_0 + \alpha_1 y_{t-1} + \alpha_2 y_{t-2} + \cdots + \alpha_n y_{t-n} + e_t$$

This says that y, industrial production, is a linear function of its own preceding values. The coefficients α_i are estimated by regressing y on its own previous values so as to find maximum correlation or minimum residual squared error:

$$\sum_{t=1}^{T} e_t^2 = \min$$

A more sophisticated and complicated expression of this approach is given by

$$y_t = \alpha_0 + \alpha_1 y_{t-1} + \cdots + \alpha_n y_{t-n} + \beta_0 x_t + \beta_1 x_{t-1} + \cdots + \beta_m x_{t-m}$$
$$+ \gamma_0 e_t + \gamma_1 e_{t-1} + \cdots + \gamma_q e_{t-q}$$

This equation is estimated by finding a best correlation of y_t with its own lagged values and with some other variable x_t (and its lags). This error structure is more complicated than the usual formulation in that it too has a lag pattern. This relation is called an *autoregressive-moving-average equation*. The autoregressive aspect is that y_t depends on its own lagged values. The moving-average aspect is indicated by the fact that a weighted combination (average) of past values of x_t and e_t are also used. This is a moving average because the items in the combination move with the passing of each time period. It is also called a Box-Jenkins relation, named after two investigators who have written extensively about its use.[3]

Simple least-squares regression analysis can be used for the pure lag correlation model with error term e_t. If the error is more complicated, say, in a moving-average representation, the methods for estimating the coefficients of the relationship involve heavier computation, much of which is described in the book by Box and Jenkins.

Strictly linear relationships, as indicated here, are not necessary, but most practice would confine itself to such a specification of the lag relationship—perhaps using logarithms instead of arithmetic values.

Survey Analysis and Forecasting

There is yet another approach to economic forecasting—through the sample-survey method. Households and firms may be approached directly and asked about their plans, hopes, or aspirations. These surveys are frequently designed to ascertain household buying plans for houses, cars, or other major consumer items. Complementary information on economic attitudes, price expectations, income status, and financial position is also ascertained. Either a direct translation of plans is used in order to predict household behavior from the outcome of such survey inquiries or relationships are established among forward-looking survey factors and major economic magnitudes measuring the state of business. Surveys may be very much up to date and relevant through the use of advanced sampling, interviewing, and tabulating techniques. Good surveying is simply a matter of staying in touch with the nation's economic pulse, with frequent field surveys, as often as every week, month, or quarter.

What is done at the household level is also done at the business firm level. Hiring plans, inventory plans, capital formation plans, and production plans are all suitable objects of investigation in regular, repeated surveys. In the case of business plans, many things have to be laid out in advance by business executives. This applies particularly to production and capital expansion plans. Indicators about these items are not mere subjective expectations, they are *commitments.*

To some extent, sample-survey specialists attempt to forecast for the economy as a whole, or strategic parts of it, with the results of repeated sample surveys alone, but survey results also can be used to good advantage in the modeling process. Investment plans are regularly introduced in the Wharton model. Consumer plans also have been used, although less successfully.[4]

The Modeling Approach

Let us now contrast the time-series approach with the modeling approach. Instead of confining the analysis to the "own" history of a particular series or to some series closely related to that series, the whole body of economic thought is brought to bear on the problem of constructing the best set of interrelationships—the number of equations being determined by the requirement that there be as many relationships as there are economic magnitudes to be estimated. A typical relationship, reduced to a two-dimensional view of it for illustrative purposes only, is that between consumer expenditures C and personal disposable income Y, both quantities being adjusted for inflation as well as seasonal variation. This relationship lies behind the S part of the construction of the IS curve in the IS-LM diagram.

Figure 1-4 illustrates the relationship, which is firmly embedded in economic theory, between C and Y. It is a fairly tight relationship, but it will be made tighter in practice by examining detailed types of consumer spending and by adding such explanatory variables as the interest rate (for the IS-LM coordinates), historical values of Y (for the dynamics), relative prices between

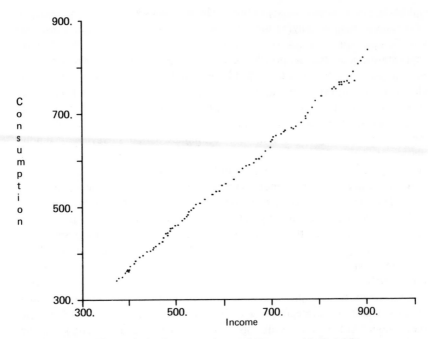

Figure 1-4. Consumption and Income, 1948-1976.

types of consumer spending (including several closely related goods), wealth measures (as distinct from income measures), and possibly necessary amounts of closely related activities.

A model may be used, in a mechanical sense, just as formal time-series relationships are used, except that the model must be solved simultaneously. In terms of Wharton models of the U.S. economy, this means solving for nearly 800 variables for the Wharton quarterly model and over 1,000 for the Wharton annual model.

There are two very significant differences which are advantageous to the modeling approach. First, there is a systematic attempt to account for the effects of specific noneconomic or externally determined variables that have important economic impacts. These variables may be determined by regular political decisions of fiscal, monetary, or technological authorities or may be separately determined in the "world" outside the model but with highly specific channels of influence on the economy. The former group constitutes *instruments* of economic policy, such as budget totals, tax rates, tax allowances, discount rates, monetary reserves, or other elements of the economy that can be altered by policy decisions. It frequently happens that the most significant changes in the economy originate among the external factors. Like the more formal time-series approach, the model-building approach is fully quantitative.

The external factors are measured and their effects on the economy are esti- mated in numerical terms. The second important difference associated with the modeling approach is that it can be used for quick studies of the effects of al- ternative economic policies. It is system designed with many instrumental policy coefficients or policy-determined variables that can be influenced greatly or even controlled by authorities. Thus the model provides a convenient quantitative framework in which to analyze alternatives. The model is useful not only in con- nection with controllable alternatives, but also in terms of speculative thinking about contingencies that can be readily studied through the vantage point of models.

The alternative economic situations with which we are likely to be con- fronted are always under scrutiny. They usually have a direct-impact component and an indirect-effect component. Without a model, it is often possible for economic analysts to come to an understanding about direct effects, but the in- direct effects come through the workings of an interrelated system. They are usually subtle and intricate. The indirect effects are often as large as or larger than the direct effects. A system of simultaneous equations is the natural way to examine and estimate these indirect effects. This is when a model is most needed.

Also, in long-run projections—the kind that are essential for investigation of such problems as energy availability, food supply, and environment and resource exhaustion—a model serves the very useful and necessary role of maintaining consistency and balance. Unless there is the formal discipline of model struc- tures, we have little assurance that the future projections, say, for the year 2000, for production, employment, imports, wage rates, etc. will all fit together. The model calculus makes a very serious attempt to impose the discipline of con- sistency on a diverse set of projected economic magnitudes.

Economists have always tried to push their reasoning beyond historical experiences. In other words, they try to extrapolate. Forecasting, in one form or another, has always been a professional challenge as well as a source of promising gain (or loss). As the subject (science) of economics developed, more and more serious scientific approaches have been tried. Chart reading and time- series analysis were among the earlier methods. These methods have undergone development and expansion. Like model building, they drew on the enormous powers of the large-scale, high-speed computer to process more series quickly, to handle complicated lag and probability (error) structures, to allow for em- pirically based interrelationships. The model approach is a more recent and, in some sense, higher form of analysis. It draws more on the analytical corpus of economic thinking. It considers more things simultaneously. It is more geared to analysis of alternatives. It is no wonder that the modeling approach has cap- tured the imagination of the economics profession and users of economic in- formation in both the private and public sectors, that it has penetrated the plans of socialist and developing-country policymakers. Indeed, the model approach is the method of our times for forecasting and policy analysis. In the chapters that follow, its main characteristics, practices, and underlying theory will be spelled out in some detail.

Notes

1. One of the most celebrated of these was by Ragnar Frisch, "Propagation Problems and Impulse Problems in Dynamic Economics," in *Economic Essays in Honor of Gustav Cassel* (London: Allen and Unwin, 1933). See also M. Kalecki, "A Macrodynamic Theory of Business Cycles," *Econometrica III*, 1935, pp. 327-344.

2. Vijaya Duggal, Lawrence Klein, and M.D. McCarthy, "The Wharton Model, Mark III; A Modern *IS-LM* Construct," in L.R. Klein and E. Burmeister (eds.), *Econometric Model Performance: Comparative Simulation Studies of the U.S. Economy* (Philadelphia: Univ. of Pennsylvania Press, 1976), pp. 188-210.

3. G.E.P. Box and G.M. Jenkins, *Time Series Analysis, Forecasting and Control* (San Francisco: Holden-Day, 1970).

4. F.G. Adams and Vijaya Duggal, "Anticipation Variables in an Econometric Model: Performance of the Anticipations Version of Wharton Mark III," in Klein and Burmeister (eds.), *Econometric Model Performance,* pp. 9-20.

2 Model Resources and Structure

Most macroeconomic models of Western industrialized economies have, at their core, elaborations of Keynesian models such as we have used for illustrative purposes. Alternative approaches have been used, but most economy-wide models have started with this approach and have evolved in the direction of more detailed structures in response to increasing demands for more disaggregation for policy analysis and forecasting.

Before discussing the econometric forecasting procedures currently in use, it is useful to survey the types of data and relationships that go into a model and the basic structure that underlies a forecasting model.

Model Data Sources

The basic data source underlying almost every economy-wide model is the National Income and Product Accounts (NIPA). Indeed, even beyond the confines of models, these accounts are generally used to measure the dimensions of an economy. When politicians, economists, or journalists refer to the "real" rate of growth, they almost invariably are referring to the rate of growth of a gross national or domestic product concept adjusted for inflation.

It is not our purpose to discuss either the history or technique of national income accounting in the United States. However, it is useful to recognize that the initial accounting scheme used for national income, the structure of early econometric models, and the concepts embodied in a Keynesian macroanalysis are all strongly interrelated. What we attempt to measure and the way we measure the economy is strongly influenced by the conceptual framework we have developed for analyzing the economy. The way in which we model the economy based on that analysis reflects in many respects the methods used for constructing the data.

Following the NIPA in constructing a model and making that set of data the foundation for forecasting has at least three advantages:

1. The NIPA are an internally consistent summary of most of the basic data sources we have for the economy.
2. They are based on an explicit theoretical construct.
3. The national income identities ensure that each segment of a forecast is consistent with others.

11

Through the National Income and Product Account, the data from retail sales reports; wage (Social Security) and income (Internal Revenue) data; employment and production statistics; financial reports of corporations; construction data; state, local, and federal budget details; foreign trade statistics; housing surveys; and numerous other basic source statistics are converted into data which describe the economy in a consistent manner. While both the flow of funds accounts and input/output data provide alternative measures of the economy, neither of these draws on sources as diverse or provides as comprehensive a summary of the economy.

In addition, both the flow of funds and input/output data are designed to describe what are intersectoral relationships. In the former case, the flow of financial claims between sectors is described, and in the latter, the flow of goods and services between industries is given. In both these accounting systems, the interest is in the gross flows between sectors. As such, they are extensions of the NIPA. The flow of funds, for example, produces a complete statement of capital accounts for individual sectors. This table is consolidated in the single capital account, entitled Gross Saving and Investment, which appears in the NIPA. The input/output table records sales from producers to producers, focusing on the way industries interact in producing the gross national product (GNP). These sales are already included in the value of the final products each sector sells and are omitted from the NIPA to avoid duplication, that is, double or multiple counting of the same transaction, in the measurement of national output.

The diversity of sources, comprehensiveness, and consistency of the accounts make them an invaluable tool for measuring the economy, but if they were not also based on a generally accepted conceptual structure, their usefulness would be substantially vitiated. At first glance, it may appear that the relevant variables are obvious, and data collection is a problem only of identifying information sources and statistical techniques. However, many issues regarding measurement depend on the theoretical relationships between variables. In particular, delineating an economy is not simply a problem of measuring conventionally existing items, but rather one of accounting for abstract phenomena.

The sense in which these measures are abstractions becomes particularly clear when an attempt is made to draw welfare conclusions from gross national product statistics. NIPA data are aggregated by weighting physical flows by prices. In a perfectly competitive market economy, these "weights" would reflect the preference orderings of individuals. Even in this case, however, the initial allocation of resources would weigh in the determination of prices and, from some social point of view, might obviate any conclusions about increasing or decreasing welfare.

A Keynesian model is a particular example of a theoretical form which can be used for specifying operational definitions for the aggregate measures we need to summarize the wealth of data generated by economic activity. Our theoretical construct could take the form of a simple Keynesian model of a closed economy such as the following:

$$Y = C + I + G \tag{2.1}$$

$$C = a_0 + a_1 Y \tag{2.2}$$

$$I = b_0 + b_1 r + b_2 \Delta Y \tag{2.3}$$

where

Y = income

C = consumption

I = investment

G = government purchases

r = interest rate

$\Delta Y = Y_t - Y_{t-1} = $ *change* in Y

Note that because we are modeling a closed economy, we neglect net exports as a component of Y in equation 2.1. This is explicitly considered later in this chapter.

This model is simply an elaboration of the I–S curve discussed in chapter 1. The relationship between the two is straightforward. Defining saving,

$$S = Y - C = I + G$$

$$S = Y - (a_0 + a_1 Y)$$

$$I + G = b_0 + b_1 r + b_2 \Delta Y + G$$

Assuming, for simplicity, that all government expenditure is investment for given values of G and Y_{t-1}, we could then trace out values for $I + G$ and S for values of r and Y. To construct the I–S curve requires that we trace out the points for which $I + G = S$ or solve for values of r and Y which satisfy

$$b_0 + b_1 r + b_2 \Delta Y + G = Y - (a_0 + a_1 Y)$$

again for given values of G and Y_{t-1}.

If Y is to represent total economic activity, then measurement within this framework should meet several obvious criteria:

1. C, I, and G should be exhaustive in their measurement of economic phenomena, with the exception of asset exchanges.

2. No activity or phenomena accounted for in one category should also appear in any other.
3. Y, C, and I should all be measured in such a way that the relationships in equation 2.2 and 2.3 are as close as possible.

While 1 and 2 may seem obvious, criteria 3 is perhaps not as straightforward. To illustrate the problem for measurement, we might consider the categorizing of expenditures on automobiles and newly constructed housing. The question is: Should these phenomena be characterized as consumption or investment? A glance at the NIPA accounting conventions yields the answer that if a household purchases an automobile, it is considered to be consumption, while if a business entity purchases it, it is treated as investment. However, purchase of a house is always assumed to be investment whether purchased by a household or a business. In part, the drawing of this distinction in the NIPA is based on considerations involving the stability and determinants of equations 2.2 and 2.3. Ideally, the distinction between consumption expenditure and investment expenditure would be drawn in a way that would minimize the error contained in these two aggregate relationships. Since, in fact, the appropriate specification for consumption and investment functions is still a matter for research, it is not possible to design an ideal set of measurement techniques. It is true, however, that the general form of the NIPA follows the broad outlines of Keynesian analysis.[2]

Given these considerations, it is not surprising that econometric models are organized in terms of the concepts embodied in the National Income and Product Accounts. But models have grown much beyond these confines. The present version of the Wharton quarterly model has fully integrated much of the basic source data from the accounts and gone beyond the basic accounts in describing the economy.

Table 2-1 is a partial listing of the types of data and sources that appear in the Wharton quarterly model. Some of these data are of interest quite apart from the NIPA. Other data have been incorporated into the model because they were found to be necessary to explain adequately elements of the NIPA itself. In addition to all the preceding, the Wharton annual model has incorporated input/output data and the Wharton quarterly model has incorporated the flow of funds data. No matter how far we range beyond the NIPA, however, the accounts and the requirement that the accounting identities must hold continue to exert a basic constraint on model design and econometric forecasting.

Model Relationships

Beyond the type and source classification just discussed, once a data series goes into an econometric model, it can be classified additionally as either exogenous

Table 2-1

Data and Sources Other than NIPA Presently in the Wharton Quarterly Model

Unit sales of automobiles	SCB[a]
Housing starts	SCB
Investment anticipations	SCB
Book value stage of process inventories	Census M3 Report
Orders and shipments	Census M3 Report
Exports and imports by SITC	FT990
Foreign exchange rates	FRB
Foreign production and price data	OECD
Interest rates	FRB
Monetary flows	FRB
Consumer and wholesale price indices	BLS, CPI, and WPI
Employment, labor force, and population	Employment and earnings
Compensation	BEA, U
Capacity utilization	Wharton
Tax rates and schedules	SOI

[a]SCB   = Survey of Current Business
FT990   = Highlights of U.S. Export and Import Trade
FRB   = Federal Reserve Bulletin
BLS, CPI = Bureau of Labor Statistics, Consumer Price Index Report
BLS, WPI = Bureau of Labor Statistics, Wholesale Price Index Report
BEA, U   = Bureau of Economic Analysis, unpublished data
SOI   = Statistics of Income
OECD   = Organization for Economic Cooperation and Development

or endogenous. An *exogenous variable* is a datum that is predetermined in the sense that its value must be specified before the model is solved and its value is not altered by the solution process. An interesting additional subdivision can be made by dividing exogenous variables into policy and nonpolicy variables. Exogenous policy variables generally include the fiscal and monetary parameters that are assumed to be under the control of government agencies and authorities. Within the Wharton models, these include government expenditures by category, tax rates, government employment, nonborrowed reserves, the discount rate, and many others. These are of special interest to forecasters because the political response to the evolving economy will weigh heavily on the accuracy of their forecasts.

Nonpolicy exogenous variables include many items that can be treated mechanically, such as seasonal indicators ("dummy" variables) and time trends, but they also encompass data which must be treated with the same care and sophistication as policy variables when forecasting. In this category fall things like exchange rates, crop conditions, and foreign industrial production. All the exogenous variables must be specified prior to attempting to solve a model or produce a forecast. As we discuss in chapter 4, a not inconsiderable part of the effort that goes into econometric forecasting is spent on developing forecasts for exogenous variables.

The set of *endogenous variables* is composed of those variables explained by the model. After we make our assumptions about what is going to happen to exogenous variables, the model determines values for these variables.

Referring to the model in equations 2.1 through 2.3, the endogenous set would include Y, C, and I, while exogenous variables would be G and r, which we can regard as measures of government fiscal and monetary policy. The assumption that G and r are exogenous is a device to simplify exposition. In a full-scale model of the U.S. economy, many components of government expenditures (for example, interest payments and unemployment transfers) will be endogenous, and the determination of interest rates will be a result of private-sector demands and public-sector supplies of monetary assets and liabilities. Even in this simple model, it is possible to draw a further distinction among endogenous variables which depends on the type of model relationship used to explain them.

Some endogenous variables are determined by identities. In this case, for example, we use the identity that income is equal to consumption plus investment plus government purchases. In a more detailed model, this would be replaced by the national income accounting identity

$$\text{GNP} = C + I + G + NE$$

where NE is net exports. Each of the categories on the righthand side of this relationship may be modeled at a more disaggregated level. In which case, they may be determined as identities themselves. Typically, exports and imports are modeled separately, or exports may be exogenous. In either case, we would then have an identity with

$$NE = \text{exports} - \text{imports}$$

In addition to the type of identity which simply requires that components of the product accounts add up, there is also a constraint imposed on the model that the income and product sides of the accounts must be equal.[3]

Other typical identities include price/quantity relationships of the sort that require, for example, that current dollar GNP be equal to constant dollar GNP multiplied by the implicit deflator. Note that when this is combined with the requirement that the GNP identity hold in both current and constant dollars, constraints are imposed on the relationship between both quantity and price components of GNP.

Equations 2.2 and 2.3 are quite different forms of relationships from the identity of equation 2.1. These equations are theoretical constructions which have unknown coefficients or parameters (a_0, a_1, b_0, b_1, b_2) which must be assigned values before the model can be solved. These parameters can be estimated using a variety of statistical techniques. Whatever method is used, however, there will be some residual error in the equation, so that, in fact, we would generally have a relationship of the form

$$C = a_0 + a_1 Y + \epsilon$$

where ϵ is a measure of the deviation of C from the value $a_0 + a_1 Y$. The ϵ term is called a *stochastic disturbance,* and relationships of this form are labeled *stochastic.* Referring to figure 1-4, it is clear that a linear relationship would fit these points very closely, and for appropriate values of a_0 and a_1, we would have only small residual error.

For estimation purposes, some assumption must be made about the behavior of ϵ, but whatever that assumption is, we desire to estimate a_0 and a_1 in a manner which will make the estimated error, a measure of the unknown and unobserved ϵ, both small and random. Some economic processes provide "tight" relationships, while others have much larger and more variable errors in any estimated equation. Consumption equations and inventory investment equations are good examples of the two extreme cases. In the former case, we should expect to find high correlation and low error variance, while in the latter, correlation is likely to be relatively low and error variance high. It would be poor econometric practice to try to force inventory equations into high correlation by using moving averages or otherwise smoothing the data we wish to explain. Our objective in this case, rather than high correlation, is to get good estimates of the parameters and random disturbances.

Stochastic relationships may themselves be categorized into various groups. The relationships in equations 2.2 and 2.3 are both behavioral. A *behavioral relationship* is one that attempts to model the response of an economic decision unit to a given set of stimuli. In general, behavioral relationships will rely heavily on economic theory and attempt to measure the response patterns to variables that economic theory indicates are relevant to the decision being made. The simple consumption relationship presented earlier, for example, is based on the Keynesian dictum that when income rises, consumption also rises. This simple model has long been abandoned for all but pedagogical purposes, but one can easily speculate about why it would not perfectly explain movements in consumption: current consumption expenditure is likely to depend both on current and expected income, consumption patterns are likely to have a certain inertia in them such that past consumption will exert an influence on present consumption; wealth as well as income is likely to influence the consumption decision; and so on. Unusual weather patterns, major political events, and many other random components may themselves exert periodic influences on the consumption decision. It is easy to see that no matter how detailed the relationship that we specify, we will never be able to account for all the phenomena that influence consumption, and some random component will always be necessary to account for the residual influences. Behavioral relationships in a macroeconomic model include those for consumption, investment, import demand, money demand, pricing, and many subcategories of these. The characteristic of each of these is that it reflects and models a decision process.

In addition to behavioral relationships, stochastic equations in an expanded macro model will include technical and institutional relationships. *Technical relationships* describe both the engineering constraints on production and the relationships among production, employment, and capacity. With the Wharton quarterly model, for example, technical relationships exist to determine the amount of output from industrial sectors necessary to produce the consumption, investment, and other final goods being demanded. To produce the worth of $1.00 of final demand for food and beverages, it will be necessary to produce output from the agricultural sector, output from the wholesale and retail trade sector, and smaller amounts from other sectors.[4] Other technical relationships exist in the form of a production function, which expresses the relationship between output and capital and labor inputs to the production process, and in relationships explaining capacity utilization based on the estimated production function.

Institutional relationships are those stochastic equations used to explain phenomena that are determined by law or custom. Among the most prominent of these are the equations which explain tax collections. The simplest form of an equation to explain personal tax collections would be

$$T = a_0 + a_1 Y + \epsilon$$

where T is collections and Y is some measure of income as a tax base. Clearly the values of a_0 and a_1 can be expected to be constant only so long as the various parameters of the tax system, including the distribution of income, tax brackets, rates, deductions, and exemptions, do not change. Variations in tax law can be expected to influence the equation parameters, and a more exact explanation of taxes would have to account for these policy variables directly.

Model Structure

Given the basic data sources and a list of variables that one wants to forecast, a wide array of models might be constructed. Special considerations involved in specifying, estimating, and validating a model to be used for forecasting are discussed in chapter 3. Issues relevant to general model construction and the broad outlines of the Wharton quarterly model are sketched in this section as a prelude to the discussion of forecasting techniques in chapter 4.[5]

Figure 2-1 is a simplified flowchart of the Wharton quarterly model which indicates the major directions of causality. It must be emphasized at the start

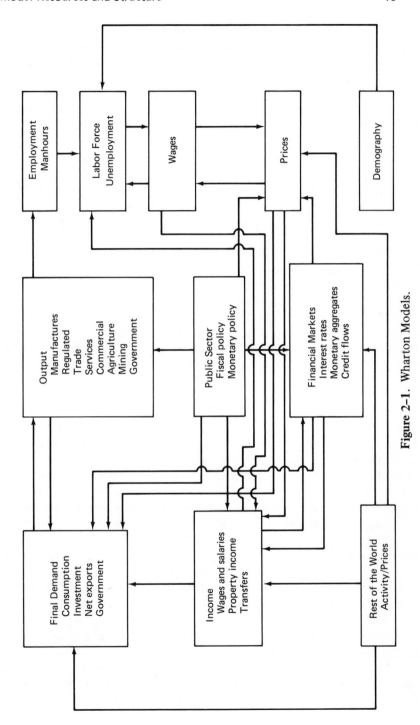

Figure 2-1. Wharton Models.

that this is a highly nonlinear dynamic system. Unlike the simple linear models used for pedagogical purposes, response characteristics will be a function both of the time path and the level of the economy, that is the stage of the business cycle. Also, as will become clear as we discuss the various components of the system, thinking of a simple causal chain, such as the one illustrated, can be edifying, but it glosses over the essential simultaneity of the system. It is true, for example, that employment at any point in time is largely determined by output, but even contemporaneously, investment by incrementing the capital stock can exert small influences on employment and over time can have quite dramatic impacts.

If primary interest is in producing a forecast or explanation of the historical path of GNP, either in current or constant dollars, one can, of course, ignore explanation of the mass of structure underlying the relationships in figure 2-1. Much simpler models have been proposed and used.[6] As we argue elsewhere, however, we believe that increased usefulness without sacrificing accuracy can be gained and, in fact, depends on detailed specification of the structure of the economy.

The following discussion is not a detailed description of individual equations or sectors of the Wharton model. To the extent that particular equations are displayed, they are intended as illustrations of the importance of economic theory and knowledge of the data base and of the major issues and problems in developing relationships that describe a simultaneous system.

Final Demand

As we indicated earlier, almost all economy-wide models have at their core a Keynesian model of the NIPA system with more or less elaboration in terms of disaggregation and detail. The fundamental problem with which the models deal is the explanation of the level of aggregate demand. The simplest place to break into the circular causal chain is in the determination of final expenditures.

The most recent version of the Wharton quarterly model includes explanations of more than fifty categories of final demand. A few of these overlap or involve alternate breakdowns of the same final demand phenomena. For example, the model explains both consumer expenditure on automobiles in value terms and unit sales of automobiles. Housing starts are explained by the model, as is residential investment expenditure. However, even allowing for this form of "double counting," it is clear that models have come a long way from early constructs that included a total of some twenty relationships to describe the entire economy.[7]

The major determinants of final demand are those suggested by economic theory. Consumption is determined by income and relative prices; investment by output, prices, and the rental rate on capital; and exports and imports by economic activity levels and prices in the United States relative to our major trading partners. Government purchases of goods and services are treated as policy decisions and are exogenously determined.

These lines of causality all appear in figure 2-1 and are the contemporaneous part of determination of final demand. What does not appear in the flowchart is the dynamic of the system which has an important impact on demand. The dynamic character of the system is captured by both lags in dependent and independent variables and the influences of stocks on contemporaneous demand decisions.

The relationship for explaining consumer expenditures on electricity and gas for household operation displayed in table 2-2 illustrates the influence of relative prices, income, system dynamics, and intersectoral impacts within the final demand sector itself. This NIPA category of expenditures is composed of expenditures on electricity and natural gas. Here the determinants of consumption are contemporaneous personal disposable income, the implicit deflator for this consumption category relative to the implicit deflator for all other consumer expenditures, and the stock of occupied residential structures. The dynamics of the system are captured by this latter term and the distributed lags on disposable income and relative prices. Both these types of dynamic relationships, distributed lags and stock effects, will require special attention when we discuss forecasting techniques.

In this relationship, we have explained expenditures on electricity and gas per unit of occupied housing as a function of relative prices and income. The effects of a change in relative prices and income occur with some delay. While a 1.0% rise in relative prices eventually can be expected to reduce consumption expenditures in this category by about 0.17% and an income change of 1.0% to increase expenditures by 0.63%, both these responses take time. The complete adjustment to an income change takes about 1 year (4 quarters), and to a price change, about 18 months (6 quarters). This slow adjustment may be attributed to a time lag in the perception of changed conditions (prices and income) by consumers or strong consumption habits that are adjusted slowly (the temperature of the house and lighting control are obvious examples). These delayed responses impart a dynamic character to the model. Moreover, past decisions concerning residential investment which determine the current housing stock also impart a dynamic behavior to the system. Other things being equal, consumption of household operating services will rise with either an increase in the housing stock or an increase in the occupancy rate of the housing stock. Given the specification we have used, we are implicitly assuming that a rise in either the stock or the occupancy rate will have a proportionate effect on expenditures. A 1.0% rise in the stock, other things equal, will cause a 1.0% rise in expenditures.

One final observation concerning this relationship is associated with the sources of the error and our ability to refine the specification of econometric

Table 2-2
Personal Consumption Expenditures, Services, Household Operation, Electricity, and Gas (Constant Dollars) = $CESSUE{+}G$[a]

$$\ln\frac{CESSUE{+}G}{NOF} = \underset{(-28.0)}{-5.4729} + \sum_{i=0}^{5} a_{i_{(2,\text{BOTH})}} * \ln\frac{PDCESSUE{+}G_{t-i}}{P1_{t-i}} + \sum_{i=0}^{3} \beta_{i_{(2,\text{BOTH})}}$$

$$* \ln YPD_{t-i}$$

where

$$P1 = \left(\frac{CE\$ - CESSUE{+}G\$}{CE - CESSUE{+}G}\right) * 100$$

$\bar{R}^2$ = 0.908
SEE = 0.025031
DW = 1.024

Period of fit: 196501 to 197604

Lag	a_i	T	β_i	T
0	−0.0178374	−2.2	0.126408	21.4
1	−0.029729	−2.2	0.189611	21.4
2	−0.0356748	−2.2	0.189611	21.4
3	−0.0356748	−2.2	0.126408	21.4
4	−0.029729	−2.2	−	
5	−0.0178374	−2.2	−	
Sum	−0.166482		0.632038	

$$NOF = (KHU1 + KHUM + KHUMH) * HOOTO * 0.01$$

$PDCESSUE{+}G$	= Implicit deflator, personal consumption expenditures on electricity and gas for household operation, 1972 = 100
$CE\$$	= Total personal consumption expenditures, billions of current dollars
CE	= Total personal consumption expenditures, billions of 1972 dollars
$CESSUE{+}G\$$	= Personal consumption expenditures on electricity and gas for household operation, billions of current dollars
YPD	= Personal disposable income, billions of 1972 dollars
$KHU1$	= Stock of single family houses, millions of units
$KHUM$	= Stock of multiple unit houses, millions of units
$KHUMH$	= Stock of mobile homes, millions of units
$HOOTO$	= Percentage of occupied year-round housing units

[a]For an explanation of equation documentation, see appendix 2A.

relationships. One obvious source of error is a failure to account for the effects of abnormal weather on expenditures. It would certainly be possible to construct a series for degree days for the United States which should help explain deviations from normal expenditures on gas and electricity for heat. By omitting this, we force deviations from "normal" weather into the stochastic disturbance.[8] This is an area where additional resources could almost certainly improve our specification and explanation by including this omitted variable.

There is, however, another obvious misspecification about which we can do little, given present data resources. The specification deals with total structures and implies that an increase in the number of mobile homes has the same impact on expenditures as an increase in the number of multiple-unit or single-unit structures. Given the differences in sizes, insulation standards, and other factors which affect energy demand, this seems unlikely, and one might wish to allow for differential impacts of these structures by including them separately on the righthand side of the equation. The problem is that the observations on the three components of structures and on income move so closely together that is is impossible to distinguish their effects when all are included as explanatory variables. We therefore use the constraint that expenditures rise in proportion to all structures as an approximation. Given a sample of data on individual households and observations on how heating expenditures varied with income and type of structure, we could perhaps estimate the appropriate set of weights to use on structures. We will return to the problem of misspecification and its impact on estimation techniques and forecasting later. It is necessary to note here only that these are not isolated instances and that all empirical work suffers from similar problems.

Output

It would be possible to deal with output as simply the sum of final demands, and indeed in early models, and in some present models, this is the path followed. Within the Wharton models, however, output, investment, prices, employment, manhours, and compensation rates are all explained at the industrial-sector level. There are twelve of these sectors in the quarterly model and fifty-four in the annual model. The industrial categories in the quarterly model are as follows:

Mining

Durable manufacturing

Nondurable manufacturing

Contract construction

Finance, insurance, and real estate

Services

Wholesale and retail trade

Agriculture

Transportation

Communications

Utilities

Government

The additional annual model categories are mainly a result of analysis of much finer detail in the manufacturing and energy sectors.

These two models also differ in the manner in which final demand is converted into output. An endogenous input/output matrix is included in the annual model.[9] This matrix is used to determine the output necessary from each industry to supply the total vector of final demand.[10] While research is underway to include a dynamic input/output matrix in the quarterly model, the present version uses a fixed matrix and averages deviations between the changes in a fixed-weight proxy for output and changes in actual output. Table 2-3 is an example of the types of relationships used to determine the level of output for a producing sector.

The relationship in table 2-3 is an example of how information outside the NIPA can be used to augment the NIPA data even when it does not directly appear in the model. While input/output data are not directly modeled, the input/output accounts are used to determine the coefficients that are used as weights for final demand categories on the righthand side of the equation in table 2-3. The input/output data trace flows of goods and services from one production sector to another and the total output of each sector. The relationship in table 2-3 determines the value added produced in any sector as a weighted sum of final demands. To get from the input/output transaction matrix to these coefficients, it is necessary to assume that the ratio of value added to gross output in each sector is a constant. This seems likely to cause problems over the business cycle. Moreover, we have here used a fixed set of weights, while the actual weights will vary as technology and relative prices change. Figure 2-2 is a graph of the levels of actual output of $XMFN$ compared with the weighted sum of final demands. As indicated, while the general behavior of actual output and the weighted sum of final demands are similar, actual output has tended to grow more quickly and exhibit more cyclical movement. The calculation for $CMFN$ shown in table 2-3 indicates that, on average, the growth rate of the two series differed by only about 0.03% a quarter over the sample period.

This formulation allows a direct measure of the effect of shifts in final demand on the industrial mix of output, which in turn affects the mix of employment and wages and has implications for total income and prices. These latter, of course, in their turn, impinge on final demand decisions.

Table 2-3
Output Originating, Manufacturing Nondurables = *XMFN*

$$\ln XMFN - \ln XMFN_{-1} = CMFN + \Delta \ln XMFNWTD$$

where *XMFNWTD* = 0.06932 * *CEDA* + 0.07256 * *CEDF* + 0.09896 * *CEDO* + 0.22287
* *CENF* + 0.26308 * *CENC* + 0.23689 * *CENG* + 0.27673 * *CENH*
\+ 0.22829 * *CENO* + 0.02447 * *CESH* + 0.02252 * *CESSUE+G*
\+ 0.03285 * *CESS-UEG* + 0.04827 * *CEST* + 0.05462 * *CESO*
\+ 0.04842 * *IBFNS* + 0.052 * *IBFNE* + 0.04842 * *IBFR* + 0.20034
* *IBIT* + 0.15474 * *TEB* −0.20155 * *TMB* + 0.0667 * *GVPF*
\+ 0.03177 * *GVPS*

CMFN   = mean (Δln*XMFN* − Δln*XMFNWTD*) = −0.00029948

Period of fit: 195902 to 197404

CEDA	= consumer expenditures on automobiles and parts, billions of 1972 dollars
CEDF	= consumer expenditures on furniture and household equipment, billions of 1972 dollars
CEDO	= consumer expenditures on other durables, billions of 1972 dollars
CENF	= consumer expenditures on food and beverages, billions of 1972 dollars
CENC	= consumer expenditures on clothing and shoes, billions of 1972 dollars
CENG	= consumer expenditures on gasoline and oil, billions of 1972 dollars
CENH	= consumer expenditures on fuel oil and coal, billions of 1972 dollars
CENO	= consumer expenditures on other nondurables, billions of 1972 dollars
CESH	= consumer expenditures on housing services, billions of 1972 dollars
CESSUE+G	= consumer expenditures on electricity and gas for household operation, billions of 1972 dollars
CESS-UEG	= consumer expenditures on other household operations, billions of 1972 dollars
CEST	= consumer expenditures on transportation services, billions of 1972 dollars
CESO	= consumer expenditures on other services, billions of 1972 dollars
IBFNS	= fixed investment in nonresidential structures, billions of 1972 dollars
IBFNE	= fixed investment in nonresidential producers' durable equipment, billions of 1972 dollars
IBFR	= fixed investment in residential investment, billions of 1972 dollars
IBIT	= change in business inventories, billions of 1972 dollars
TEB	= U.S. exports of goods and services, billions of 1972 dollars
TMB	= U.S. imports of goods and services, billions of 1972 dollars
GVPF	= federal government purchases of goods and services, billions of 1972 dollars
GVPS	= state and local government purchases of goods and services, billions of 1972 dollars

*Employment, Employee Hours, Labor Force,
and Unemployment*

Given the level of output necessary to support the vector of final demand, total employee hours and employment by industry sector are determined by a labor-requirements relationship derived from an inverted production function. The estimated relationships for nondurable manufacturing appear in table 2-4. Both

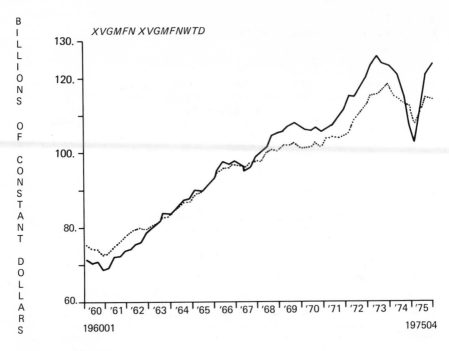

—— Actual Output
----- Computed Output

Figure 2-2. Relationship between Actual and Computed Output Originating, Manufacturing Nondurables.

these relationships can be derived from a Cobb-Douglas production function in the following manner:

$$X_t = Ae^{\delta t} L_t^{*\alpha} K_t^{\beta} e^{ut} \tag{2.4}$$

$$\ln L_t^* = \alpha^{-1} \ln X_t - \alpha^{-1} \ln A - \alpha^{-1}\beta \ln K_t - \alpha^{-1}\delta t - \alpha^{-1}u_t \tag{2.5}$$

$$\Delta \ln L_t = \lambda(\ln L_t^* - \ln L_{t-1}) \tag{2.6}$$

$$\Delta \ln L_t = \lambda\alpha^{-1} \ln X_t - \lambda\alpha^{-1} \ln A - \lambda(\ln L_{t-1} + \alpha^{-1}\beta \ln K_t) - \lambda\alpha^{-1}\delta t - \lambda\alpha^{-1}u_t \tag{2.7}$$

where L_t^* = "equilibrium" labor input

K_t = capital input

X_t = output

For both employment and employee hours, it is assumed that movement toward

Table 2–4
Employee Hours, Nondurable Manufacturing = *NMLTTMFN*

$\Delta \ln NMLTTMFN = -0.0499058 + 0.261644 * \ln XMFN -0.237243 * (\ln NMLTTMFN_{-1}$
$ (0.42) \quad\quad (7.25) \quad\quad\quad\quad\quad (6.75)$

$ + 0.32279 \ln KIAMFN) - 0.00136852 * DUMTIME$
$ (4.81)$

where $\bar{R}^2 = 0.424$
$ SEE = 0.0079$
$ DW = 1.097$

Period of fit: 1954.1 to 1973.4

Employees on Nonagricultural Payrolls, Nondurable Manufacturing = *NEETTMFN*

$\Delta \ln NEETTMFN = -0.126210 \quad - 0.000778233 * DUMTIME + 0.135565 * (1.1029$
$ (-9.02446) \quad\quad (-8.36855) \quad\quad\quad\quad (9.01704)$

$ * \ln XMFN - \ln NEETTMFN_{-1} - 0.32279 * \ln KIAMFN)$

$\bar{R}^2 = 0.509$
$SEE = 0.0045881$
$DW = 1.092$

Period of fit: 1953.4 to 1973.4

KIAMFN = Nondurable manufacturing capital stock, billions of 1972 dollars
DUMTIME = Time trend, 1948, first quarter = 1
XMFN = Output originating in nondurable manufacturing, billions of 1972 dollars

---

the equilibrium labor input can be described by the partial adjustment mechanism specified in equation 2.6.

If the production process exhibited constant returns to scale, that is, if $\alpha + \beta = 1$, it is possible to demonstrate that for the cost-minimizing competitive firm, $\alpha^{-1}\beta$ would be the equilibrium ratio of the capital income share to the labor share. While the production process is not constrained to exhibit constant returns to scale, $\alpha^{-1}\beta$ is estimated by averaging income shares over the sample period. Moreover, the employee hours and employment relationships are constrained to lie on the same long-run production surface, except for a scalar which accounts for average weekly hours.

The function explaining hours at the top of table 2-4 is based on equation 2.7 with $\alpha^{-1}\beta$ estimated as the average of the ratio of income shares over the sample period. In addition to this constraint, in the employee equation, the constraint that α and β take the same values as the estimated values in the hours equation also has been imposed. This results in constraining the coefficient on ln *XMFN* to equal α^{-1}, estimated by dividing the estimate of λ into the estimate of $\lambda\alpha^{-1}$ in the hours equation. In the employee equations, the only estimated parameters are λ, δ, and a scale factor with

λ = speed of adjustment

δ = rate of technological change plus the change in the average work week

It should be noted that the estimated speed of adjustment λ is greater in the hours equation than in the employees equation. This conforms to what is thought to be normal industrial practice.

The relatively low levels of the multiple correlation coefficient for these relationships sometimes cause concern about the explanatory power of the equations. In both cases, the dependent variable is the change in logarithms. Change variables have greater dispersion than level variables, and explanatory power is seldom as great as in level relationships. When this equation is solved for the actual level of manhours, the estimated and actual data are very close.

The supply side of the labor market is determined by the labor force participation rate equation in table 2-5. The major determinants are the employment rate (*NEHT/NPTN*16+) and the real wage rate. Minor effects are caused by the level of the Armed Forces, the proportion of the population accounted for by males between the ages of 25 and 34, and the cyclical movement of real per capita income. In this relationship, the dynamics arise from the notion that the participation decision depends on the expected return from entering the labor force. That return will depend on the expectation of finding a job, which is determined by the distributed lag on the employment rate, and the expected real wage, which is determined again by a distributed lag. A further discussion of this relationship appears at the end of this chapter.

Compensation and Prices

Compensation rates in most industries are determined by a relationship of the type illustrated in table 2-6. This is a modified version of what is known as the Phillips curve,[11] in which the rate of change of wage rates is inversely related to the unemployment rate. The explanation of the rate of change of wages has been modified in several respects from a simple Phillips curve. First, in addition to the level of the unemployment rate, the rate of change of the unemployment rate and the inflation rate were added to the explanation of wage rate increases. An additional modification is necessary because the variable being explained is compensation rather than wage rates.

In addition to wage payments, compensation includes employer contribu-

Table 2-5
Total Labor Force = NLT

$$NLT/NPTN16+ = 0.266975 + 1.53544 * (NLTMA25.34*/NPTN16+) + 0.340287$$
$$(6.31) \qquad (2.92) \qquad\qquad\qquad\qquad (2.22)$$

$$* (NLM/NPTN16+) - 0.496426 * [YPDPC/YPDPC_{-1} * 0.98^0$$
$$(2.50)$$

$$+ YPDPC_{-2} * 0.98^1 + YPDPC_{-3} * 0.98^2 + \cdots + YPDPC_{-15}$$

$$* 0.98^{14})] + \sum_{i=1}^{3} a_{i(2,\text{FAR})} * (NEHT/NPTN16+)_{t-i} + \sum_{i=1}^{3}$$

$$b_{i(1,\text{FAR})} * [(NLTMA25.34*/NPTN16+) * (NEHT/NPTN16+)]_{t-i}$$

$$+ \sum_{i=2}^{9} c_{i(2,\text{BOTH})} * [(WBC\$ - WBCAG\$ - WBCGV\$ - SUPTE\$)/$$

$$NMLTTPV/PDCE * 100]_{t-i}$$

$\bar{R}^2 = 0.957$
$SEE = 0.0015780$
$DW = 1.527$

Period of fit: 195904 to 197404

Lag	a_i	T	b_i	T	c_i	T
1	0.245758	4.45	−0.835902	1.64	−	−
2	0.163838	4.45	−0.557268	1.64	0.000905795	4.57
3	0.0819192	4.45	−2.78634	1.64	0.00158514	4.57
4	−	−	−	−	0.00203804	4.57
5	−	−	−	−	0.00226449	4.57
6	−	−	−	−	0.00226449	4.57
7	−	−	−	−	0.00203804	4.57
8	−	−	−	−	0.00158514	4.57
9	−	−	−	−	0.000905795	4.57
Sum	0.491515		−1.67180		0.0135869	

$NPTN16+$	= total noninstitutional population, 16 years and over, millions
$NLTMA25.34*$	= total male labor force, ages 25 to 34, millions
NLM	= armed forces, millions
$NEHT$	= employed persons, millions
$PDCE$	= implicit deflator, total consumer expenditures, 1972 = 100
$YPDPC$	= disposable income per capita, billions of 1972 dollars
$WBC\$$	= total compensation of employees, billions of dollars
$WBCAG\$$	= employee compensation in agriculture, forestry, and fisheries, billions of dollars
$WBCAGV\$$	= employee compensation in government and government enterprises, billions of dollars
$SUPTE\$$	= employer contributions for social insurance
$NMLTTPV$	= private nonagricultural sector manhours, billions per year

Table 2-6

Compensation Rate, Manufacturing Nondurables = $WRCMFN\$$

$$[(WRCMFN\$ - WRCMFN\$_{-1}) - (SUPTE\$/NMLTTPV - SUPTE\$_{-1}/NMLTTPV_{-1})]$$

$$/WRCMFN\$_{-1} = \sum_{i=0}^{5} a_{i_{(1,FAR)}} * (1.0/NRUT)_{t-i} * \left\{ 1.0 - [(SUPTE\$_{-1} \right.$$

$$/NMLTTPV_{-1})/WRCMFN\$_{-1}]\right\} + \sum_{i=0}^{4} b_{i_{(2,FAR)}} * [(PDCE$$

$$- PDCE_{-1})/PDCE_{-1}]_{t-i} * \left\{ 1.0 - [(SUPTE\$_{-1}/NMLTTPV_{-1}) \right.$$

$$/WRCMFN\$_{-1}]\right\} + \sum_{i=2}^{6} * c_{i_{(1,FAR)}} [(NRUT - NRUT_{-1})$$

$$/NRUT_{-1}]_{-i} * \left\{ 1.0 - [(SUPTE\$_{-1}/NMLTTPV_{-1})/WRCMFN\$_{-1}]\right\}$$

$\bar{R}^2$ = 0.517
SEE = 0.0050610
DW = 1.631

Period of fit: 195304 to 297702

Lag	a_i	T	b_i	T	c_i	T
0	0.00781124	6.50	0.179862	1.49	–	–
1	0.00650951	6.50	0.225803	7.04	–	–
2	0.00520761	6.50	0.230788	5.53	−0.00833591	2.77
3	0.00390571	6.50	0.194816	3.12	−0.00666872	2.77
4	0.00260380	6.50	0.117886	2.40	−0.00500154	2.77
5	0.00130190	6.50	–	–	−0.00333436	2.77
6	–	–	–	–	−0.00166718	2.77
Sum	0.0273399		0.949155		−0.0250077	

$SUPTE\$$ = employer contributions to social insurance, billions of dollars
$NMLTTPV$ = total private manhours, billions of hours
$NRUT$ = unemployment rate
$PDCE$ = implicit deflator, consumer expenditures, 1972 = 100

tions for social insurance. Clearly this component of compensation is not responsive to labor market conditions but is established by legislative fiat.

Letting WRC equal compensation per manhour, W equal wage per hour, S equal employer contributions to social insurance, and $\dot{X}$ the time derivative of X, then

$$WRC = W + S \tag{2.8}$$

$$W\dot{R}C = \dot{W} + \dot{S} \tag{2.9}$$

$$\frac{W\dot{R}C}{WRC} = \frac{\dot{W}}{W}\frac{W}{WRC} + \frac{\dot{S}}{WRC} \tag{2.10}$$

or

$$\frac{W\dot{R}C - \dot{S}}{WRC} = \frac{\dot{W}}{W}\frac{WRC - S}{WRC} = \frac{\dot{W}(1 - S)}{W\ WRC} \tag{2.11}$$

Letting

$$\frac{\dot{W}}{W} = \sum_{i=1}^{q} \alpha_i \frac{1}{u} + \sum_{i=1}^{n} \beta_i \frac{\dot{u}}{u} + \sum_{i=1}^{m} \frac{\dot{p}}{p}$$

where u = unemployment rate

p = price

and substituting into equation 2.11 we can derive a form which in discrete terms is the estimated function.

In addition, compensation rates for certain industrial sectors are based on their relationship to manufacturing compensation rates rather than labor market conditions directly.

There are three major sets of price indices incorporated in the Wharton quarterly model. The basic set of prices is made up of the implicit deflators for output originating from industrial sectors. These are modeled as behavioral equations on the assumption that firms maximize the expected value of discounted profits based on the production process described by the production function estimated in the hours-employment sector and facing a well-defined demand curve. It is possible to demonstrate that under these conditions the firm will set its price as a markup over a geometrically weighted average of factor input prices, with the weights determined by the parameters of the production function.[12] The behavioral relationship illustrated by table 2-7 is based on this result. The variable *COSTMFN* is described as the logarithm of a geometric average of unit labor costs and unit capital costs. In each case, the cost measures have been estimated by averaging productivity or price measures over a period sufficient to eliminate sharp cyclical shifts. The price responses to these cost measures are in turn assumed to occur over time through the distributed lag on *COSTMFN*. Note also that cyclical variation in the markup over

Table 2-7
Implicit Deflator, Output Originating, Nondurable Manufacturing = PXMFN

$$\ln PXMFN = 4.34857 + \sum_{i=0}^{3} a_{i(1,FAR)} COSTMFN_{-i} + \sum_{i=0}^{3} b_{i(2,FAR)} CUN1_{-i}$$

$$+ 0.979 * U_{-1}$$

Lag	a_i	T	b_i	T
0	0.142029	7.41276	0.0000568624	0.177090
1	0.106521	7.41276	0.000536599	4.05320
2	0.0710143	7.41276	0.000687034	3.71752
3	0.0355072	7.41276	0.000508168	3.13842
Sum	0.355072		0.00178866	

$\bar{R}^2$ = 0.994
SEE = .0058345
DW = 0.045

Period of fit: 1955.1 to 1973.4

$$COSTMFN = 0.90674 * \ln\left[WRCMFN\$ / \frac{1}{12} \sum_{i=0}^{11} \left(\frac{XMFN}{NMLTTMFN} \right)_{-i} \right] + 0.292687$$

$$* \ln\left(\frac{KIAMFN + KIAMFN_{-1}}{2.0 * XMFN} \right) * \left[\left(\frac{1}{4} \sum_{i=1}^{4} UCKMFN_{-i} \right)\right]$$

CUN1 = 1/[1 − (CUWIPMFN + CUWIPMFN_{-1})/200]
UCKMFN = rental rate on capital
CUWIPMFN = capacity utilization in nondurable manufacturing
XMFN = output originating in nondurable manufacturing, billions of 1972 dollars
KIAMFN = nondurable manufacturing capital stock, billions of 1972 dollars
NMLTTMFN = employee hours, nondurable manufacturing
WRCMFN$ = compensation rate, manufacturing nondurable

cost is captured by the nonlinear term in capacity utilization. The assumption here is that capacity utilization reflects the demand conditions facing the firm.

The other two types of prices that appear in the Wharton quarterly model are the implicit deflator for final demand categories and components of the wholesale and consumer price indices. The determination of each of these is based on what are essentially technical relationships regarding production. Tables 2-8 and 2-9 illustrate the general forms of these equations. Implicit deflators for final demand are based on the fact that the value of final demand is the sum of value added in the production process. This is the transpose of the

Table 2–8
Implicit Deflator, Personal Consumption Expenditures, Nondurables, Other Nondurables = PDCENO

$$\ln PDCENO - \ln PDCENO_{-1} = CPCENO + \Delta \ln PDCENOWTD$$

where $PDCENOWTD = 0.06608 * PXAG + 0.01977 * PXMG + 0.00651 * PXCC + 0.22829$
$\qquad * PXMFN + 0.08343 * PXMFD + 0.04069 * PXRGT + 0.01306$
$\qquad * PXRGC48 + 0.01476 * PXRGU49 + 0.40309 * PXWR + 0.05567$
$\qquad * PXFI + 0.05197 * PXSV + 0.01302 * PXGV - 0.00889$
$\qquad * PTMEGTCM - 0.00525 * PXRW$
$\qquad CPCENO = \text{mean} (\Delta \ln PDCENO - \Delta \ln PDCENOWTD) = -0.00011008$

Period of fit: 195902 to 197404

PXAG	= implicit deflator for output originating in agriculture, 1972 = 100
PXMG	= implicit deflator for output originating in mining, 1972 = 100
PXCC	= implicit deflator for output originating in contract construction, 1972 = 100
PXMFN	= implicit deflator for output originating in nondurable manufacturing, 1972 = 100
PXMFD	= implicit deflator for output originating in durable manufacturing, 1972 = 100
PXRGT	= implicit deflator for output originating in transportation, 1972 = 100
PXRGC48	= implicit deflator for output originating in communication, 1972 = 100
PXRGU49	= implicit deflator for output originating in utilities, 1972 = 100
PXWR	= implicit deflator for output originating in wholesale and retail trade, 1972 = 100
PXFI	= implicit deflator for output originating in finance, insurance, and real estate, 1972 = 100
PXSV	= implicit deflator for output originating in services, 1972 = 100
PXGV	= implicit deflator for output originating in government, 1972 = 100
PTMEGTCM	= unit-value index for crude materials imports, 1972 = 100
PXRW	= implicit deflator for output originating in rest of the world

---

relations illustrated in table 2-3, where final demand quantities determine output quantities. Conceptually, a dollar of final expenditure represents a dollar of value added, and it is possible to assign the value added to the firms or industry producing it. Working from this type of relationship, it is possible to demonstrate that the implicit deflator for any category of final demand will be a weighted average of the implicit deflators for value added for the industries that have contributed to producing the product, with weights determined by the proportion of the real output that the industries contribute.

For example, let

$\qquad F\$_j$ = total expenditure on final demand of type j
$\qquad\qquad$ (current dollars).

$\qquad F_j$ = total expenditure on final demand of type j
$\qquad\qquad$ (constant dollars).

Table 2-9

Wholesale Price Index, by Processing, Crude Materials, Not Seasonally Adjusted = $PWPC^*$

$PWPC^* = -1.13437 + 0.807817 * \ln PFR^* + 0.181769 * \ln PTMEGTCM + 0.104593$
      (8.13)   (30.53)   (2.74)   (2.38)

      $* \ln PXMG + 0.00739397 * DUMSA01 + 0.00892231 * DUMSA02 + 0.00614706$
           (1.24)   (1.49)

      $* DUMSA03$

$\bar{R}^2$ = 0.982
SEE = 0.018581
DW = 0.380

Period of fit: 195401 to 197304

U.S. Consumer Price Index, Rent, Not Seasonally Adjusted = $PCSR^*$

$(PCSR^*/PCSR^*_{-1} - 1.0) * 100.0 = 0.0719474 * (PXFI/PXFI_{-1} - 1.0) * 100.0 + 0.0841501$
                       (1.63091)   (4.13526)

      $* (PXCC/PXCC_{-1} - 1.0) * 100.0 + 0.175682$
                   (4.96784)

      $* (PXRGU49/PXRGU49_{-1} - 1.0) * 100.0 + 0.129025$
                         (2.01252)

      $* (PXSV/PXSV_{-1} - 1.0) * 100.0 + 0.0137115$
                  (3.06448)

      $* \left(1.0/[1.0 - (HORIO + HORIO_{-1})/200.0] \right)$

$\bar{R}^2$ = 0.638
SEE = 0.19919
DW = 0.903

Period of fit: 1956.3 to 1973.4

PFR^*	= index of prices received by farmers, 1910–1914 = 100
$PTMEGTCM$	= unit-value index, U.S. general imports, crude materials, 1972 = 100
$PXMG$	= implicit deflator, output originating in mining 1972 = 100
$DUMSA01, DUMSA02, DUMSA03$	= seasonal dummy variables
$PXFI$	= implicit deflator, output originating in finance, insurance, and real estate, 1972 = 100
$PXCC$	= implicit deflator, output originating in contract construction, 1972 = 100
$PXRGU49$	= implicit deflator, output originating in utilities, 1972 = 100
$PXSV$	= implicit deflator, output originating in services, 1972 = 100
$HORIO$	= percent of occupied housing units

PF_j = implicit deflator for final expenditure of type j.

$X\$_{ij}$ = value-added contribution of industry i to final expenditure of type j (current dollars).

X_{ij} = value-added contribution of industry i to final expenditure of type j (constant dollars).

PX_i = implicit deflator for value added from industry i.

By definition,

$$PF_j = \frac{F\$_j}{F_j}$$

And if we assume that all output of industry i carries the same price $PX_i = X\$_{ij}/X_{ij}$ for all j, then

$$F\$_j = \sum_i X\$_{ij}$$

$$F_j = \sum_i X_{ij}$$

$$PF_j = \frac{F\$_j}{F_j} = \frac{\sum_i X\$_{ij}}{\sum_i X_{ij}} = \sum_i \frac{X\$_{ij}}{\sum_i X_j} = \sum_i \frac{X_{ij}}{\sum_i X_{ij}} \frac{X\$_{ij}}{X_{ij}}$$

$$= \sum_i \omega_{ij} PX_i$$

where $\omega_{ij} = \dfrac{X_{ij}}{\sum_i X_{ij}}$

If ω_{ij} were known for all j, implicit deflators for final demand categories would simply be identities. Since we do not know the value of ω_{ij} at each point in time, and since the appropriate deflator for industry value added may vary among final expenditure categories, we cannot use this type of identity. As illustrated in table 2-8, we have followed a procedure similar to that used in determining output originating. The relationship between this and output determination is clear when it is noted that the weight on *PXMFN* in determining *PDCENO* is the same as the weight on *CENO* in determining *XMFN* in table 2-3; that is, one set of relationships is the transpose of the other. Figure 2-3 shows the relationship between *PDCENO* and the weighted average of output prices.

The final set of prices in the model include the wholesale price index, the consumer price index, components of these two, and miscellaneous price indices

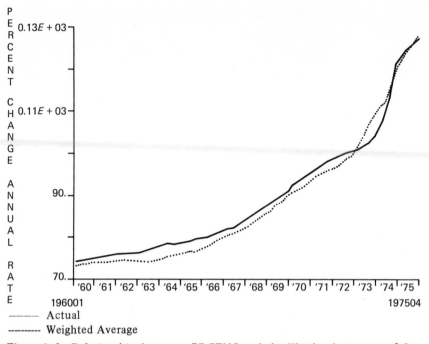

Figure 2-3. Relationship between *PDCENO* and the Weighted Average of Output Prices.

which are not necessary for any of the basic accounting identities but are closely related to them. This group of indices is explained by relating them to other price indices that are components of the desired index and/or to market conditions that will affect them. Two of the prices in this group appear in table 2-9.

Income Determination

The explanation of the income side of the NIPA is often given cursory treatment in econometric models. From a forecasting point of view, however, a well-specified sector for the determination of income components is very important, because data on these components are available earlier in the quarter than most other data, because preliminary data in certain of the personal income categories tend to be revised less than in product categories, and because of the strong feedbacks into the product side through the determination of personal disposable income.

In actual accounting practice, the total on the income side of the NIPA is reconciled with the product side of the accounts through a statistical discrepancy. This is essentially a residual used to enforce the identity that final product must equal the factor income that results from producing that product. When using a model, several options are available for ensuring that this identity holds. One of these is simply to follow accounting practice, letting total GNP be determined by the product side of the accounts, explaining the components of the income side, and allowing the residual to be determined as the discrepancy between the two. Within the Wharton quarterly model, we do allow total GNP to be determined by the product side of the accounts, but the value of the statistical discrepancy is determined exogenously, and the residual item used to reconcile income and product totals is corporate profits. The discrepancy will often move in a surprising way on short notice, swinging by more than $5.0 billion between two successive quarters. This type of movement can have a dramatic impact on profits forecasts and result in large errors.

We have already discussed the major determinants of the largest single item on the income side of the accounts, wage and salary disbursements. These payments account for approximately one-half of GNP and two-thirds of personal income. Given compensation per hour and hours worked, total compensation is simply the product of the two. To get from compensation to wage and salary payments, it is necessary only to subtract supplements to wages and salaries and wage accruals less disbursements. The former is an endogenous variable, and the latter is exogenous to the model.

Other major components of personal income—proprietors income, rental income, dividends, personal interest income, and transfers—are determined either by behaviorally or institutionally based stochastic relationships or identities. For example, dividends are modeled as a choice function of corporations based on current cash flow and past dividend policy. Rental income is a function of the consumer price index (CPI) for rent and the capital stock of housing, with modifications both for the fact that rental income is net of expenses, while the CPI for rental services includes such expenses, and for the fact that a large component of net rental income is an imputation for owner-occupied housing. Transfer income is the sum of federal, state, and local and business transfer income.

It is necessary not only to determine these income flows to people, but also the other items that delineate the income side of the accounts, such as capital consumption allowances, indirect business taxes, business transfers, the statistical discrepancy, and subsidies less current surplus of government enterprises. These items enable one to get from GNP to net national product to national income. If we have fully determined the elements of personal income, the final step is reconciling the difference between national and personal income. As noted earlier, in the Wharton model this is accomplished by determining all the reconciling items except profits, which is the residual item on the income side of the accounts. Clearly, the profit residual depends heavily on the value assigned to the statistical discrepancy. One could argue that a better residual concept is corporate profits plus the statistical discrepancy. However, this residual measure is of limited interest to users of model forecasts.

Perhaps the single most important item on the income side of the accounts, from the point of view of the accuracy and reliability of the model, is the determination of personal disposable income, which is the most important determinant of consumer expenditures. Personal disposable income is simply personal income less personal tax and nontax payments. While the state and local component of these tax payments is determined by one institutional type regression relationship, the federal sector is elaborated in considerable detail, including eleven regression relationships, two identities, and ten exogenous variables which describe the rate structure and exemptions.

Financial Markets

Financial variables are an important and integral part of the Wharton quarterly model. Interest rates and financial flows influence consumer expenditures on durable goods, residential and nonresidential investment, income flows, and prices. The core of this sector is the determination of the key short-term interest rate. Other short-term and long-term rates are then based on their relationship to this key rate. Financial stocks and flows, such as currency in the hands of the public, private demand deposits, time deposits, free reserves, large certificates of deposit, stock of commercial and industrial loans, and consumer credit, are modeled as the demand or supply side of the respective markets.

The key short-term rate in the Wharton quarterly model is the rate on 4- to 6-month commercial paper. For estimation purposes, the relationship which determines this rate within the model is specified as a demand for private deposits normalized on the interest rate. Several constraints are imposed on the estimated relationship with respect to the speed of adjustment in reaction to changes in determinants of demand and the elasticity of demand with respect to interest rates. The upper half of table 2-10 is the specification of the demand function in which the speed of adjustment is constrained to be 0.3, and the elasticity of demand with respect to the time deposit rate *FRMBPE* is constrained to be twice the elasticity with respect to the commercial paper rate. The lower half of the table is the estimated version of the equation, which, in turn, is solved for *FRMCP4M* within the model.

Public Sector

The final segment of the model is the public sector. This is interpreted in a broad sense to include not only federal, state, and local entities but also the monetary authorities. While much of this sector is determined by exogenous policy variables, some important aspects are endogenous to the model. As mentioned in the discussion of income determination, the explanation of federal personal income taxes involves eleven regressions, two identities, and specification of ten exogenous variables. Table 2-11 lists the exogeneous variables which describe

Table 2-10
Interest Rate on 4- to 6-Month Dealer-Placed Commercial Paper = *FRMCP4M*

$\ln FDBDP\$/XP\$ - 0.3 * \ln(FDBDP\$_{-1}/XP\$_{-1}) = \alpha_0 + \alpha_1\ [2 * \ln(1.0 + 0.01 * FRMBPE)$

$+ \ln(1.0 + 0.01 * FRMCP4M)] + \alpha_2$

$\ln GNPPCPEAK + \alpha_3 \ln(FRMDNY$

$$/FRMDNY_{-1}) + \sum_{i=0}^{5} \alpha_{4+i}[\ln XP_i$$

$/XP_{-1-i}) - \ln(XP_{-1-i}/XP_{-2-i})]$

$2 * \ln(1.0 + 0.01 * FRMBPE) + \ln(1.0 + 0.01 * FRMCP4M)^{\text{a}} = -1.06423\qquad -0.247872$
$\qquad\qquad\qquad\qquad\qquad\qquad\qquad\qquad\qquad\qquad\qquad (-7.80597)\quad (-5.51377)$

$* \ln(FDBDP\$)/XP\$) - 0.3$

$* \ln(FDBDP\$_{-1}/XP\$_{-1})$

$+ 0.0774654 * \ln$
$\quad (2.06985)$

$GNPPCPEAK + 0.0512616$
$\qquad\qquad\qquad (3.90788)$

$* \ln FRMDNY/FRMDNY_{-1}$

$$+ \sum_{i=0}^{5} a_i DLNXDOT_{-i}$$

Lag	a_i	T
0	-0.340115	-3.94961
1	-0.451637	-6.46714
2	-0.495876	-6.34713
3	-0.472832	-5.69774
4	-0.382504	-5.21258
5	-0.224894	-4.87920
Sum	-2.36786	—

$\bar{R}^2$ = 0.949
SEE = 0.0096389
DW = 0.654

Period of fit: 1955.1 to 1975.4

$$DLNXDOT = \ln(XP/XP_{-1}) - \ln(XP_{-1}/XP_{-2})$$

FRMBPE	= effective interest rate on passbook savings at commercial banks
FDBDP$	= private demand deposits at commercial banks
GNPPCPEAK	= peak value of per capita GNP
FRMDNY	= discount rate, Federal Reserve Bank of New York
XP$	= GNP originating private sector, billions of dollars
XP	= GNP originating private sector, billions of 1972 dollars

[a]This equation is solved for *FRMCP4M* for forecasting.

Table 2-11
Exogenous Public-Sector Variables

Federal

FDBDG$	= U.S. government demand deposits at commercial banks
GVGIA$	= grants-in-aid to state and local governments
GVPFD$	= defense purchases of goods and services
GVPFO$	= nondefense purchases of goods and services
GVPTGDAV$	= federal government purchases of automobiles
GVSUBTF$	= subsidies less current surplus of federal government enterprises
ITRA	= effective investment tax credit rate, by industry
LNT	= effective tax life of equipment and structures, by industry
NEETTGVF	= federal government employees
NLM	= Armed Forces
ORNACGD$	= new orders for defense capital goods
TEBGTEDOD$	= exports under U.S. military agency sale contract
TMBDE$	= imports direct defense expenditures
TRGFPRES$	= U.S. federal government transfers to persons other than unemployment insurance benefits
TXCBFOIL$	= indirect business taxes on crude oil imports
TXCSTP$/TXCSTT$	= ratio of employee contributions of social insurance to total
TXOPFEV$	= statutory exemption for federal personal income tax
TXOSMAXY$	= maximum earned income subject to social security tax
TXRBTEFBC	= index of U.S. import duty rate
TXRGF	= federal tax on gasoline per gallon
TXRITE	= effective corporate tax rate, by industry
TXRITNF	= statutory marginal corporate profits tax rate
TXRPTNFY	= personal income tax rate, first nine brackets by bracket
TXRSTEF	= effective social security tax rate
WBSGVFGDM$	= military wages and salaries
WRCGVFG$	= federal general government compensation per man year, including military

State and Local

GVSUBTS$	= subsidies less current surplus of state and local government enterprises
GVPS$	= state and local purchases of goods and services
NEETTGVS	= state and local employees
TRGSP$	= state and local transfer payments to persons
TXRBTESRES	= effective tax rate for state and local indirect business taxes
TXRGS	= state and local gasoline tax
WRCGVSG$	= state and local compensation per man year

Monetary Authorities

FBFASSO$/O+B$	= proportion of Federal Reserve holdings of other U.S. securities to total
*FREN$**	= nonborrowed reserves
FRMBPC	= maximum interest rate payable on passbook saving accounts
FRMCDC	= maximum interest rate payable on large certificates of deposit
FRMDNY	= discount rate, New York Federal Reserve Bank
FRRED	= effective reserve requirement, demand deposits
FRRET	= effective reserve requirement, time deposits

Not Elsewhere Classified

XGVE$	= output originating in federal, state, and local enterprises

public-sector behavior. Once this set of variables has been specified, relationships within the model determine the public and private sectors, including tax collections, surplus/deficit positions, interest rates, and monetary aggregates. Both figure 2-1 and table 2-11 indicate that the public sector impinges on the economy and the model not only by its direct influence through traditional policy instruments such as total expenditures and tax collections, but also through the composition of those instruments.

Keynesian Analysis and Econometric Models

As we noted earlier, most of the major econometric models in use are Keynesian in orientation. The term *Keynesian* can mean many things—from the simplest textbook example of income-expenditure determination to large-scale models with fully articulated supply and demand relationships interacting with each other. Our longer-run Wharton model used for decade projections even combines a complete input/output system with detailed relationships that determine income and expenditure flows. In any event, whether we are making short-run quarterly analyses or longer-term annual projections, this discussion of specification should make it clear that supply side effects are not ignored. Our models are very different from the type of Keynesian analysis which has been criticized as ignoring incentives and supply considerations.

Unfortunately, the term *supply* is used very loosely, even by professional economists. Technically, the *supply* of a factor of production, or any commodity or service, is the amount that would be offered for any specified values for prices, incomes, tastes, and other relevant determinants. Economists have traditionally been most concerned with variations in the supply of any item when its *own* price changes. With respect to recent policy discussions, the issues are whether econometric models properly account for the determinants of the primary factors of production, labor, and capital. Beyond this issue, there is a larger question on the production side regarding the description of the supply of intermediate goods and services and of primary commodities such as agricultural and mining products.

Within the framework of the Wharton econometric models, the supply of labor and capital to the production process is determined by the statistical relationships which explain the labor force participation rate and the investment decisions of firms. Because these relationships are embedded in a large model, much of the impact of policy changes on the supply of labor and capital is indirect, and the casual observer may be misled into concluding that it does not appear. Moreover, there is room for improvement in these measures, and we would not assert that all incentive effects have been captured. We would, however, raise the question of the quantitative impact of those which are not included in the model.

As noted earlier, to explain the size of the labor force, individuals are assumed to decide to enter or not to enter the labor market based on the real wage per hour that is being offered, the employment rate, and the level of their real disposable income relative to what might have been expected based on past growth trends. These three components generally attempt to measure movements in the wage individuals can expect to earn if they get a job, the possibility of finding a job, and whether income is high or low compared with past income levels.

The first two terms are estimated to have a positive impact on the labor force. If the real wage or the employment rate rises, more people begin to look for work in the expectation both of a higher probability of finding a job and of earning more if employment is secured. The income effect on participation is negative. That is, for a given real compensation rate and a given employment level, an increase in real disposable income, say, by way of a tax cut, will lower the labor force participation rate since at higher income levels, individuals choose to consume more leisure and less in the way of additional goods. This phenomenon is generally recognized in the literature on labor markets. Cyclically, it can be accounted for as the impact on secondary workers who enter the labor force to maintain family income when real family incomes decline and leave when incomes return to customary levels. Secularly, it might be interpreted as a backward-bending supply curve for labor with respect to income, and it might be used to explain the decline in participation of prime-age males over the last decade.

Policy decisions can affect this relationship in many ways, but there are two major channels through which a personal tax cut would influence the decision to enter the labor force. First is the immediate impact on disposable income of a personal tax cut. Increasing after-tax incomes results in a lower participation rate than otherwise would have occurred. Second, the increase in purchases of goods and services which follows a tax cut results in an increase in the employment rate, which in turn acts to increase the labor force. Which of these influences predominates depends very much on the conditions under which taxes are cut and the size of the reduction.

If the economy is in a cyclical trough with low employment and low incomes, the employment effect will generally be greater. As employment and incomes rise, the reverse is likely to be true. Moreover, at a cyclical peak with high employment and incomes, both these effects may be overwhelmed by wage changes. Since the determinant of labor force participation is the real wage rate, the impact on participation depends on whether wages or prices rise more quickly. At cyclical peaks, our estimates are that wage changes occur relatively rapidly, and a tax cut would be expected to increase real compensation and participation. At low levels of economic activity, effects on real compensation may be dominated by the effects of the employment rate and income changes.

There is an additional tax impact via the determination of real compensation rates, since these are determined by correcting employee compensation by an inflation factor, using a price index that includes indirect business taxes. A reduction in these taxes would have the effect of increasing real wages and attracting additional workers to the labor force. Therefore, we do take account of both direct and indirect taxes in determining labor supply in the Wharton econometric model, contrary to many assertions that the supply side is overlooked.

With respect to the supply of capital, it is assumed that business investment is determined on the basis of the profitability of any investment project. This means that the cost of any investment must be weighed against the expected after-tax earnings which that investment would be expected to provide and yields on alternative investments. The level of the corporate profits tax, the investment tax credit, interest rates, prices of capital goods, expected product prices, and expected sales all enter the calculation.

A reduction of the corporate profits tax or an increase in the investment tax credit acts to increase the after-tax return on any investment and increases the aggregate level of investment. There are, however, secondary effects from such a reduction that may act to offset some of the increase. An increase in investment may lead to increases in the price of capital goods. The increase in the government deficit may lead to higher interest rates as the Federal Reserve acts to control growth in monetary aggregates. Other effects act to reinforce the initial stimulus as rising incomes generated by the additional investment act to increase sales. Again, which effect predominates depends crucially on the situation of the economy when the policy initiative occurs.

While the determinants of the supply of primary factors of production have been the focus of recent policy discussions, an additional dimension on the suppy side which is important in the analysis of policy is the flow of intermediate products through the producing sectors of the economy. These flows can have major implications for inflation and production near cyclical peaks as some sectors begin to approach maximum production levels and either create production bottlenecks or fuel inflation with rapid price increases. The Wharton annual model has an endogenous input/output matrix which allows us to predict these flows for over fifty producing sectors. Under varying policy assumptions, it is possible to monitor the price and production implications of any policy on an industry basis, including not only the demand for primary factors of each industry, but the demand and supply of intermediate goods.

Perhaps the weakest sector on the supply side of macroeconomic models is the explanation of the supply of primary commodities. The effects of tax incentives or penalties on the production of petroleum and natural gas are obvious areas where the models are weak. But even here, progress is being made. The Wharton agricultural model projects the production of a wide array of livestock and commodities and is solved in conjunction with the Wharton macroeconomic models to evaluate policy impacts on agricultural output and prices. We have developed an alternative version of the Wharton annual model which explains both production and consumption of energy in great detail and has been used to project production of petroleum, natural gas, and coal.

Summary

This cursory description of the Wharton quarterly model is indicative of the knowledge of data, economic theory, and economic institutions necessary to specify and estimate a macroeconomic model. As a final caveat, it should be recognized that the current version of this model, and the situation in macroeconomic modeling in general, is in a state of flux. Research is constantly underway to improve the explanation of economic phenomena already incorporated in the model and to elaborate and extend the analytical capabilities both for forecasting and for policy analysis. Any model is an approximation to the economy of the real world. Our best approximation always leaves room for improvement as new data, new thinking about the economy, new institutions, greater computer power, and *experience* guide us to the next effort.

Econometric models have proven to be useful adjuncts to both business and government policy decisions, but they must be used with care and understanding of their limitations as well as their strengths.

Notes

1. For historical development, see C.S. Stine, "The History of the United States National Income and Product Accounts: The Development of an Analytical Tool," Ph.D. dissertation, George Washington University, 1971. A description of techniques can be found in *Survey of Current Business, National Income Supplements,* 1954 and 1958; August 1965 and January 1976.

2. For a detailed discussion of these points, see Charles Leven, "Social Accounts: Theory and Measurement," Chapter 15, in Paul Davidson and Eugene Smolensky, *Aggregate Supply and Demand Analysis* New York: (Harper and Row, 1964).

3. Strictly speaking, the income and product sides of the accounts will differ by the statistical discrepancy which must be determined in some fashion. In the Wharton quarterly model, this is exogenous. A further GNP identity not discussed in the text must hold for the Wharton models, since output originating by sector is also modeled. For a discussion of these data, see J.J. Gottsegen and R.C. Zemer, "Comparison of Federal Reserve and OBE Measures of Real Manufacturing Output, 1947-64," in J.W. Kendrick (ed.), *The Industrial Composition of Income and Product* (New York: NBER, 1968).

4. Within the Wharton quarterly model, this translation is based on fixed coefficients estimated from input/output data. Within the Wharton annual

model, the translation is accomplished using a fully embedded input/output system (see the discussion to follow in the text).

5. It is not our intent to give a detailed description of model structure or estimates. The interested reader is referred to M.D. McCarthy, *The Wharton Quarterly Econometric Forecasting Model, Mark III* (Philadelphia: Univ. of Pennsylvania, 1972), for a description of an earlier version of the Wharton quarterly model. A description of the more recent structure is in preparation.

6. See L.C. Andersen and J.L. Jordan, "Monetary and Fiscal Actions, A Test of Their Relative Importance in Economic Stabilization," *Federal Reserve Bank of St. Louis Monthly Review,* November 1968; and Ray C. Fair, "An Evaluation of a Short-Run Forecasting Model," in L.R. Klein and E. Burmeister (eds.), *Econometric Model Performance* (Philadelphia: Univ. of Pennsylvania, 1976).

7. See, for example, L.R. Klein, *The Keynesian Revolution,* 2d ed. (New York. Macmillan, 1966), chapter 9.

8. Note that only deviations from the mean go into the disturbance, since the average impact appears in the constant term.

9. For a full description of this technique, see R.S. Preston, "The Wharton Long-Term Model: Input-Output within the Context of a Macro Forecasting Model," *International Economic Review* 16, no. 1, February 1975, reprinted in Klein and Burmeister (eds.), *Econometric Model Performance.*

10. For a description of input/output, see *Survey of Current Business* 43, February 1974, pp. 24-56.

11. See A.W. Phillips, "The Relation Between Unemployment and the Rate of Change of Money Wage Rates in the United Kingdom, 1862-1957," *Economica* 25, November 1958, pp. 283-299.

12. See W.D. Nordhaus, "Recent Developments in Price Dynamics," in O. Eckstein (ed.), *The Econometrics of Price Determination* (Washington: Board of Governors of the Federal Reserve System, 1972).

Appendix 2A
Interpretation of
Equation Documentation

A general equation takes the form

$$Y = \underset{(t_{a0})}{a_0} + \underset{(t_{a1})}{a_1 * X1} + \underset{(t_{a2})}{a_2 * X2_{-1}} + \underset{i=0}{\overset{3}{\sum}} \underset{(NP)}{a_{3+i} X3_{-i}}$$

where:

Lag	a_i	T
0	a_3	t_{a3}
1	a_4	t_{a4}
2	a_5	t_{a5}
3	a_6	t_{a6}

Sum $\underset{i=3}{\overset{6}{\sum}} a_i$

$\bar{R}^2 =$

$SEE =$

$DW =$

t_{ai} = t statistic for test of the null hypothesis that $a_i = 0$

$\bar{R}^2$ = coefficient of determination, corrected for degrees of freedom

SEE = standard error of estimate

DW = Durbin-Watson statistic

(NP) indicates that the distributed lag was estimated using an Almon polynomial:

N = degree of the polynominal

P = (FAR, NEAR, BOTH, NONE), indicating constraints placed on the polynomial to be equal to zero at the period (1) beyond the farthest period of the lag variable, (2) before the lag begins, (3) both, or (4) none of these

Detailed explanation of these statistics can be found in any introductory econometrics text.

3

Specification and Validation of a Forecasting Model

Any problem which is subjected to econometric analysis, whether it is testing a hypothesis, explaining history, or forecasting, is composed of steps which can be classified into

1. Specification
2. Estimation
3. Validation
4. End use

Our contention is that when the end use is a forecasting model, whether it is a generalized economy-wide model or a model of firm, industry, or product sales, certain issues must be confronted with respect to specification, estimation, and validation that may be ignored in many more academic exercises.

Specification involves the problem of translating hypotheses about the determinants of economic phenomena into estimable relationships. At the optimum it draws heavily on both economic and statistical theory. At a minimum it is supported by a grab bag listing of all the variables that might be related to the one of primary interest. The problems involve the appropriate mathematical relationships, dynamics, and stochastic specification. Some of the effects of economic theory, data, and statistical theory on specification were illustrated in chapter 2, but it is not our purpose to discuss the general specification problem. There are, however, considerations particularly relevant to developing a forecasting model that are often not appreciated in a more general context of econometric modeling and which affect the usefulness of a model for forecasting.

The issue of estimation techniques appropriate or justifiable for use in conjunction with economy-wide models has been the subject of extensive research and is clearly related to specification as well as end use. Without concerning ourselves with the technical issues involved in this problem, we comment on the fact that for the foreseeable future, large models are likely to continue to be estimated mainly by ordinary least squares, and the potential problems this raises for validation beyond the problems of the statistical properties of the estimator.

Finally, we concern ourselves with the issues of validating a statistical model whose intended end use is forecasting.

Specification Issues for Forecasting Models

In developing a model to be used for forecasting economic phenomena, the specification that is used will occasionally be dictated by the particular process being considered, by the data set that describes it, or by generally accepted principles established in modeling similar phenomena. In general, however, a variety of alternative specifications will be admissible, and standard statistical tests either will not be applicable or will not be able to discriminate among them. While each forecasting problem will have many aspects that are unique to it, certain decisions involving choices among admissible specifications have to be made about almost all models, and these ultimately affect the difficulty and accuracy of forecasting. Among the most important of these are decisions regarding

1. Level of aggregation
2. Degree of exogeneity
3. Amount of structural detail

While the discussion of these issues is cast in terms of macroeconomic models, the same issues arise in models of industries, regions, product sales, and virtually all other economic models.

Aggregation

The maximum level of aggregation is typically dictated by the decision environment in which the model will be used.[1] That maximum level will be determined by the point at which the aggregation process means that use of the model in fact yields no incremental information for decision purposes. For example, if the problem is to determine the impact on teenage unemployment of a 1.0% decline in aggregate unemployment, then a model which explains only aggregate unemployment will not yield useful information until it is augmented or extended to explain the link between aggregate unemployment and teenage unemployment.

Every model is an approximation to the unknown, but true, underlying system of the economy. Models estimated at different levels of aggregation are different approximations of the same system. One approximation may be traded for another because of the presence of some disaggregated information that is deemed particularly relevant.

While for countercyclical policy purposes it may be sufficient to explain the response of the aggregate unemployment rate to a policy action, for social policy purposes it may be necessary also to explain the unemployment rate for teenagers, women, blacks, and other demographic categories. For a firm's investment decision, the precision with which investment and production decisions can be made will increase as the level of disaggregation approaches its own product line sales. For energy policy analysis, it may be necessary not only to know the total amount of output, but also its composition for purposes of predicting final energy demand. In each of these cases there is some necessary minimum level of disaggregation before the forecast data become relevant to the decision process. Intuitively, one feels that gains and losses in accuracy of estimates and forecasts will offset one another at some level of disaggregation, but no well-developed theory exists concerning the determination of that level.

It is worth noting that elimination of aggregation error as it is generally discussed in economics is not one of the advantages of disaggregation. The error that results from aggregation and the conditions under which it is possible to obtain "consistent" aggregation have been well documented.[2] The problem from an estimation and forecasting point of view relates to the stability of the parameters of aggregate relationships. If, for example, we are interested in relating aggregate consumption to aggregate income

$$C = a + bY + \epsilon$$

where $C = \sum_{ij} c_{ij}$

$$Y = \sum_{j} Y_j$$

$j = 1, ..., s$ (households)

$i = 1, ..., m$ (goods)

and we postulate that the underlying relationships at the household level are of the form

$$c_{ij} = a_{ij} + b_{ij}Y_j + \epsilon_{ij}$$

then

$$C = \sum_{ij} c_{ij} = \sum_{ij} a_{ij} + \sum_{ij} b_{ij}Y_j + \sum_{ij} \epsilon_{ij}$$

$$= a + \tilde{b}Y + \epsilon$$

where $\tilde{b} = \dfrac{\sum_{ij} b_{ij}Y_j}{\sum_{j} Y_j}$

If $b_{ij} = b_i$ so $\tilde{b} = \sum_i b_i$ or if $Y_j = \alpha_j Y$ so $\tilde{b} = \sum_{ij} b_{ij}\alpha_j$, the aggregate coefficient will be constant. In general, however, the aggregate coefficient will depend both on the distribution of income across households and on marginal propensities to consume across both goods and households. Even if the latter were constant but not identical across individuals, shifts in income distribution would affect the mean parameter value of the aggregate relationship. Similar types of problems arise with almost all aggregation and become more severe when dealing with non-linear relationships.

For this case, disaggregation across goods will not avoid the problem. The gains in disaggregating for estimation purposes are to be found, if at all, in the ability to deal with specific effects that are difficult to assess at the aggregate level and which one hopes will average out when aggregated. Specifics in the consumption area would be the effects of relative prices and the substitutability or complementarity of various goods. A finer specification should result in more precise estimates and allow for a description of the underlying interaction of the system.

For example, purchases of gasoline will depend not only on income and relative price, but also on the time path of automobile purchases. In turn, the purchase of automobiles will depend on the price of gasoline. At a disaggregated level we can estimate this interrelationship. Moreover, when we use this model for forecasting purposes if we are confronted with a proposed OPEC oil price increase, we need estimate only the impact on gasoline prices and the model should indicate the impact on automobiles and gasoline demand.

This general type of advantage could be classified as an ability to refine structural specification. A model which explains the components of consumption at a disaggregated level can take into account factors that will not appear to be significant at the aggregate level. The example of gasoline and automobiles has already been mentioned. Another example might be the relationship between new housing and consumer expenditures on household durable goods such as furniture and appliances. If the stock of occupied housing units rises, this should increase expenditure on household durables, even if incomes are the same,[3] as people purchase new appliances and furnishings.

In addition to specification advantages, disaggregation is likely to allow greater precision in the estimation of the dynamic structure of the model. The effort that econometricians have devoted to estimating distributed-lag relationships has largely been aimed at alleviating the problems of loss of degrees of freedom and multicollinearity that specification of such a relationship raises. It is well known that n first-order difference equations can generally be reduced to one nth-order difference equation. Let us suppose that we can explain movements in y_1 by the following dynamic system:

$$y_{t1} = y_{t2} + y_{t3} \tag{3.1}$$

$$y_{t2} = \alpha y_{t-1,2} + \epsilon_{t2} \tag{3.2}$$

$$y_{t3} = \beta y_{t-1,3} + \epsilon_{t3} \tag{3.3}$$

We can estimate this disaggregated system or substitute y_{t2} and y_{t3} out of the system to work with a higher level of aggregation. Substituting equations 3.2 and 3.3 into equation 3.1 yields

$$y_{t1} = \alpha y_{t-1,2} + \epsilon_{t2} + \beta y_{t-1,3} + \epsilon_{t3} \tag{3.4}$$

Lagging equation 3.1 one period and multiplying by α with some rearrangement we can derive

$$\alpha y_{t-1,2} = \alpha y_{t-1,1} - \alpha y_{t-1,3}$$

Similarly,

$$\beta y_{t-1,3} = \beta y_{t-1,1} - \beta y_{t-1,2}$$

and from equation 3.4

$$\begin{aligned} y_{t1} &= \alpha y_{t-1,1} - \alpha y_{t-1,3} + \epsilon_{t2} + \beta y_{t-1,1} - \beta y_{t-1,2} + \epsilon_{t3} \\ &= (\alpha + \beta) y_{t-1,1} - \alpha y_{t-1,3} - \beta y_{t-1,2} + \epsilon_{t2} + \epsilon_{t3} \end{aligned} \tag{3.5}$$

Again from equations 3.2, 3.3, and 3.1,

$$-\beta y_{t-1,2} = -\beta \alpha y_{t-2,2} - \beta \epsilon_{t-1,2}$$
$$-\alpha y_{t-1,3} = -\alpha \beta y_{t-2,3} - \alpha \epsilon_{t-1,3}$$
$$-\alpha \beta y_{t-2,1} = -\alpha \beta (y_{t-2,2} + y_{t-2,3})$$

Combining these last three expressions,

$$\begin{aligned} -\alpha y_{t-1,3} - \beta y_{t-1,2} &= -\alpha \beta (y_{t-2,2} + y_{t-2,3}) - \beta \epsilon_{t-1,2} - \alpha \epsilon_{t-1,3} \\ &= -\alpha \beta y_{t-2,1} - \beta \epsilon_{t-1,2} - \alpha \epsilon_{t-1,3} \end{aligned}$$

and substituting this into equation 3.5, we get

$$y_{t1} = \alpha^* y_{t-1,1} + \beta^* y_{t-2,1} + \epsilon^*_{t1} \tag{3.6}$$

where $\alpha^* = \alpha + \beta$

$\beta^* = -\alpha\beta$

$\epsilon^*_{t1} = \epsilon_{t2} + \epsilon_{t3} - \beta \epsilon_{t-1,2} - \alpha \epsilon_{t-1,3}$

The aggregated system (equation 3.6) will have a longer distributed lag, and estimation of it will require resort to distributed-lag estimation techniques, which generally require additional computational resources and/or some a priori assumption concerning the shape of the lag structure.

In addition to easing the problem of estimation of distributed-lag relationships, we expect disaggregation to have some impact on the forecast error of the system. Intuitively, the hoped-for gains can be illustrated by simply examining the difference between forecasting aggregate income Y_t on a single relationship basis and as the sum of its components, say, consumption C_t, investment I_t, and government purchases G_t. In the first instance,

$$Y_t = \tilde{Y}_t + \epsilon_{yt}$$

where $\tilde{Y}_t$ indicates the forecast value of Y, and ϵ_{yt} is the forecast error. For the disaggregated approach, we have

$$Y_t = \tilde{C}_t + \tilde{I}_t + \tilde{G}_t + \epsilon_{Ct} + \epsilon_{It} + \epsilon_{Gt}$$

Clearly the relative accuracy of the two approaches to forecasting is going to depend on the relative variances and deviations from zero of ϵ_{yt} vis-à-vis $\epsilon_{Ct} + \epsilon_{It} + \epsilon_{Gt}$. There is some intuitive appeal to the notion that disaggregation allows one to spread the risk and average errors. We may, by increasing the precision of specification, be able to reduce the variances such that we expect the following (neglecting covariances among components C, I, and G):

$$\sigma^2_{\epsilon_y} > \sigma^2_{\epsilon_C} + \sigma^2_{\epsilon_I} + \sigma^2_{\epsilon_G}$$

where the variances σ^2_i are single-equation forecasting error variances. Even if this is not true, covariances among the forecast errors for C, I, and G, when the disaggregated approach is used, may reduce the variance of the forecast error relative to an aggregate relationship. This may occur if covariances among the forecast errors of the disaggregated categories are predominantly negative. In our example, the formula for variance of y, aggregated from $C + I + G$ is

$$\sigma^2_{\epsilon_y} = \sigma^2_{\epsilon_C} + \sigma^2_{\epsilon_I} + \sigma^2_{\epsilon_G} + 2\sigma_{\epsilon_C \epsilon_I} + 2\sigma_{\epsilon_C \epsilon_G} + 2\sigma_{\epsilon_I \epsilon_G}$$

where the last three terms on the righthand side are covariances between the errors of components of y. Clearly, if the sum of these is negative, it enhances the possibility that disaggregation will result in greater forecasting accuracy.[4]

It is, of course, true that the hoped-for reduction in forecast error when disaggregation occurs may be illusory. Moreover, while we have argued that disaggregation can be expected to allow more precision in specification and estimation through a more accurate or detailed picture of the interrelationships of the economy that would bring with it more flexibility in analyzing policy problems, these advantages are not purchased without cost.

More detail obviously imposes additional problems of data acquisition and control. It also presents greater opportunity for misspecification. In general, one expects that the greater the number of equations which need to be estimated, the higher will be the probability of making a substantive specification error in one of them. The effects of specification error on the properties of estimators have been well documented.[5] The forecasting properties of a model will reflect the properties of the estimators. For example, if we use the relationship $y_t = a + bX_t$, where a and b are estimated, to forecast y, such that $y_t^f = a + bX_t^f$ when the true relationship is $y_t = \alpha + \beta X_t + \gamma Z_t$, we obtain the following expression for forecast error:

$$y_t^f - y_t = a + bX_t^f - \alpha - \beta X_t - \gamma Z_t$$
$$= (a - \alpha) + bX_t^f - \beta X_t - \gamma Z_t$$

Adding and subtracting βX_t^f on the righthand side yields

$$y_t^f - y_t = (a - \alpha) + (b - \beta)X_t^f - \beta(X_t - X_t^f) - \gamma Z_t$$

If we assume that X_t^f is an unbiased forecast of X_t, independent of b, and that both X_t and Z_t are nonstochastic, then

$$E(y_t^f - y_t) = [E(a) - \alpha] + [E(b) - \beta]X_t - \gamma Z_t$$

That is, we will expect error based on the bias in the estimated coefficients as a result of misspecification and the effects of the omitted variable. If y, in turn, is a determinant of other variables in the system, misspecification of this single equation is likely to affect the entire forecast.

In addition to greater data requirements and an increased opportunity for introducing specification error, disaggregation increases the costs of using a model for forecasting and policy analysis. There is the obvious cost of more resources required for solving the model, but the greater cost is associated with acquiring an understanding of the working of a system necessary for either forecasting or decision analysis. As will become clear when we discuss the mechanics of producing a forecast, a great deal of judgment is involved in using an econometric model for forecasting. Much of this judgment must be based on a knowledge of the interrelationships of the model being used. While one hopes to get a closer approximation of economic reality by modeling the complex relationships among economic variables and attempting to trace as many of these as possible, it does lead to a structure that is necessarily more complicated and more difficult to control. As a general rule, using a large, complex model efficiently and effectively will require a greater commitment of resources but should also yield the benefit of greater flexibility and precision. Table 3-1 summarizes the expected gains and losses of disaggregation.

Table 3–1
Gains and Losses from Disaggregation

Estimation	
Gains	*Losses*
More precise specification	Increases chance of specification error
Shorter lag structure in disaggregated equations	Larger data requirement

Forecasting	
As above, plus finer detail for analysis	As above, plus more cumbersome structure to control
Possibility of favorable variance/covariance structure	
Diversification and spreading of bias	

Exogeneity

Given a set of parameter estimates, the solution to any econometric model through time, whether it is a single linear relationship or a large system of equations, will depend on the values taken by the exogenous variables and, if the system is dynamic, the set of initial conditions.[6] While this is obvious, the importance this assumes in comparing two models or in specifying a model for forecasting purposes is often overlooked.

A simple example might illustrate the problem. Suppose that the behavior of the economic phenomena in which we are interested can be described by the following recursive set of relationships:

$$y_{t1} = \alpha_0 + \alpha_1 y_{t2} + \alpha_2 X_t + \epsilon_{t1} \tag{3.7}$$

$$y_{t2} = \beta_0 y_{t-1,1} + \epsilon_{t2} \tag{3.8}$$

If the variable of ultimate interest is y_{t1}, then three approaches to estimating this system are available. First, equation 3.7 may be estimated as a single relationship, assuming y_{t2} to be exogenous to the system. Second, the equation set 3.7 and 3.8 may be estimated together. Finally, we could substitute equation 3.7 out of the system and estimate the following reduced-form equation:

$$y_{t1} = \alpha_0 + \alpha^*_1 y_{t-1,1} + \alpha_2 X_t + \epsilon^*_{t1}$$
$$\alpha^*_1 = \alpha_1 \beta_0 \quad \epsilon^*_{t1} = \epsilon_{t1} + \alpha_1 \epsilon_{t2} \tag{3.9}$$

Any of these procedures could produce estimates with desirable statistical properties from an estimation point of view, but they have different implications for required resources and usefulness in forecasting exercises.

If equation 3.7 is estimated as a single equation, it will be necessary to supply projections of the variables y_{t2} and X_t over the forecast horizon in order to use the model for forecasting y_{t1}.

If either the set of equations 3.7 and 3.8 or equation 3.9 is used to forecast y_{t1}, the information requirement for y_{t2} over the forecast is eliminated and only X_t and an initial value for $y_{t-1,1}$ is required for forecasting. The difference between these two is the ability the former provides to monitor the feedback process through y_{t2}.

Notice also the difference in comparing these models on the basis of within-sample simulations, a strategy that is often used in comparing models for the purposes of selecting one for forecasting. In the first case, historical simulation will simply reproduce the residual errors from the least-squares regression equation. In the second case, simulation of the system dynamically and simultaneously allows error to enter the system both in terms of the estimation error and because both contemporaneous and historical values are produced by the system. The value of y_{t2} used in determining y_{t1} will not be the actual value used in estimation but the value predicted by equation 3.8. Once the system is used to predict more than one period into the future, additional error may accumulate because the values for $y_{t-1,1}$ used to predict y_{t2} will be solution rather than historical values. Similar comments apply to case 3. The point to be recognized here is that in order to approximate a valid test of two forecasting systems which differ in their degree of exogeneity, it would be necessary to attempt to approximate the methodology that will actually be used in projecting exogenous variables for forecasting purposes.

In a general context, the degree of exogeneity of contemporaneous variables determines how much the forecast is determined by judgmental forces and how important model structure is to the forecast. It is not only the number of exogenous variables that is important, but the type of variable. The impact of judgment on the forecast is clearly minimized the greater the proportion of exogenous variables that can be mechanically updated or are unlikely to stray from a predetermined level over the forecast horizon. In this class would be time trends, certain population variables, and some policy variables which either generally have long lead times for alteration, such as certain aspects of the federal tax code, or are determined by disaggregated behavior which results in stability of trends, such as the effective excise tax rate for the state and local sector. Unfortunately, many of the variables that one feels should be exogenous to the system, such as federal expenditures and monetary policy, are very much a matter of judgment concerning both political feasibility and expediency and cannot adequately be forecast either as trends or by assuming that government projections will be realized. Additionally, one is confronted with the problem of choosing a point at which variables which clearly are going to be affected by variables that are endogenous to the system are exogenized because an adequate explanation of their behavior would go beyond the bounds of resource availability. A glaring example present in most U.S. macroeconometric models is the assumption that the world economy is exogenous to behavior of the U.S. economy. At the industry or regional level, one is often forced into making assumptions about the general level of the economy in order to solve a model of the steel or automobile industry or of a state or region whose behavior, in fact, may have a dramatic impact on the variables which are exogenized.

Specification decisions at this margin can alleviate or impose burdens on the forecasting exercise. These may be with regard to external information acquisition. Also, the forecaster must himself develop feedback from the forecast to what might be termed *semiexogenous* variables. If the U.S. economy is expected to exhibit slow growth, for example, it is unlikely that world trade will achieve high levels of activity, and assumptions must reflect this. Additionally, it is necessary to make some judgment concerning the likely policy response to the forecast evolution of the economy. This latter problem becomes particularly severe when the forecast goes beyond a 6- to 8-quarter horizon.

A final point to be noted here is the limitation that the type and number of exogenous variables put on alternative scenarios. As we discuss elsewhere, one of the great advantages of using a model for forecasting purposes is the facility it provides in exploring "what if" types of questions. Generally, these involve changing one or more of the exogenous variables or shocking an endogenous variable. As discussed here and elsewhere, however, one of the methods used to evaluate the validity of exogenous assumptions is the impact they have on the forecast. To the extent that the exogenous set is "tuned" to the forecast, changing a few without reevaluating the entire set is likely to result in a misstatement of alternative results.

Simultaneity/Structure

As is typical in working with large systems, when to a large degree everything depends on everything else, the specification problems of aggregation, exogeneity, and simultaneity/structure are very much related to each other, and many of the points made earlier relate to the problem of the amount of structural detail which is desirable in a forecasting model. As an illustration of the problem consider the choice between a model consisting of equations 3.7 and 3.8 or of equation 3.9.

The case for structural, as opposed to reduced-form, estimates in models to be used for forecasting and policy analysis was forcefully stated by Marschak 26 years ago.[7] Marschak argues that a knowledge of structure is necessary when among the alternatives being considered for policy purposes is a policy which would alter the structure. The nature of the argument can be exemplified very simply. If the personal tax structure has been stable over a period of time in terms of rate structure, exemptions, deductions, and so on, it would be possible to relate personal tax collections to personal income by a relationship such as

$$\ln T = a_0 + a_1 \ln YP\$$$

where, given the progressive nature of the tax structure, we would expect $a_1 > 1$. This type of relationship is likely to work quite accurately in forecasting over a period in which no changes in the tax structure are expected to occur. However, if the parameters of the tax system are expected to be altered, one is confronted with the problem of adjusting the values produced by the equation to reflect this change, since the parameters of the estimated equation reflect the current tax structure.

It may be possible, and indeed it is typically true, that when a tax alteration is proposed, calculations can be made by government economists to evaluate its differential impact on collections. However, to evaluate each proposal accurately can be a laborious process, and quite often the impact on collections of the alteration in the general economy caused by the tax change is overlooked or underestimated.

The ability to evaluate quickly and consistently the effects of such proposals is increased by incorporating the structure of the tax system in a model of the entire economy so that an alteration in rates or deductions can be evaluated by changing the appropriate parameters of the tax system, say, the level of tax rates by tax class or the value of the standard deduction. Clearly the most desirable state of affairs would be to include each type of deduction, exemption, and special category in such a way that one could simply alter the appropriate tax parameter and solve for the impact on collections, the federal deficit, and the rest of the economy. One is confronted with a choice between the great detail that maximizes flexibility and the costs of manageability of data and model problems. While one acknowledges the correctness of the position that structure is desirable, at some point, the increased accuracy and flexibility one hopes to derive from increased structural detail is offset by increasing data demands and the increased difficulty of analyzing a model which includes a wealth of detail.

An alternative to a structural approach to a forecasting model is a reduced form. As noted, we can exemplify this choice by that between the system of equations 3.7 and 3.8 and equation 3.9. Both these systems can be used to forecast values for y_{t1} through time. Both require X_t as exogenous inputs to the system to do a forecast. The difference in these two systems lies only in the explicit dependence of y_{t1} on y_{t2} in the former case.

The choice between these two systems must rest largely on the desirability of monitoring the relationship between y_{t1} and y_{t2}. If the relationship between y_{t1} and $y_{t-1,1}$ in equation 3.9 is perceived to have altered because, say, one observes postsample errors substantially larger than those which within-sample statistics would lead one to expect, the alteration may be the result of misspecification or structural shift, for example, in either equation 3.7 or equation 3.8. If both equations have been estimated and are included in the model, then it is possible to isolate the source of the error for further investigation.

The resolution of the specification question is going to vary substantially between models constructed for differing purposes or based on different prior conceptions of structural relationships. How these decisions affect the problems of evaluation and comparison of models is a topic of ongoing research and debate.

Estimation and Validation Issues for Forecasting Models

Conceptually, estimation and validation issues can be treated separately, but present validation techniques are strongly related to the estimation techniques in use for estimating large models. It is therefore useful to consider these two issues jointly.

While much effort has been devoted to the question of estimating economy-wide models by using appropriate methods of simultaneous-equation-systems estimation,[8] for a variety of reasons, large models are commonly estimated using single-equation ordinary least squares (OLS) despite the well-known statistical problems of consistency. While more sophisticated methods are theoretically appealing from a statistical point of view, most large models have not been estimated using full-information methods, such as three-stage least squares or full-information maximum likelihood. The problem is that the number of behavioral relationships in these models is greater than the number of data points available for estimation. The sample-error covariance matrix is singular under these conditions. While one version of the Wharton model was estimated using two-stage least squares (2SLS) and sectors of other models have been estimated using full-information simultaneous methods,[9] even 2SLS requires some modification since the number of observations is generally less than the number of exogenous variables, which leads to singularity of the moment matrix for reduced-form evaluation.

Even if these problems were not present, it seems likely that heavy reliance would continue to be placed on single-equation OLS in estimating large models. The reasons for this include the apparent sensitivity of full-information estimators to misspecification, the nonlinearities which appear to be essential in many relationships, and the frequency with which single equations are modified or added to the model. Data revisions and changes in model structure lead us to reestimate part or all of a model with a frequency that would make elaborate estimation methods burdensome.

This use of OLS raises severe problems for validating econometric models.[10] Even if one had a set of well-behaved estimates of the system parameters, the problem of generating system-specific goodness-of-fit measures and test statistics is generally unresolved.[11] Given the properties of the OLS estimates, that is, that they can be expected to be inconsistent and biased, the typical methods used for validating models are examination of simulation properties, multiplier analysis, and forecasting results.

The major point to be recognized in validating forecasting models is that there are no generally recognized methods of statistical inference available. What we discuss here is a brief survey of current practice, and what should be clear is that accepting a model as a useful forecasting tool is still largely a matter of good judgment. The validation methods are quantitative and descriptive, but they are not generally based on probability calculations from established distributions.

Simulation and Multiplier Analysis

Simulation analysis basically consists of solution of the model or some subsector of the model with actual historical or assumed values of the variables exogenous to the subsector. A simple dynamic model of consumption, investment, and GNP will serve to illustrate most of the issues. Suppose the model in which we are interested takes the following form:

$$Y_t = C_t + I_t + G_t$$
$$C_t = a_0 + a_1 Y_t + a_2 C_{t-1}$$
$$I_t = b_0 + b_1 r_t + b_2 \Delta Y_t$$

where Y_t = income

C_t = consumption

I_t = investment

G_t = government purchases

r_t = interest rate

$\Delta Y_t = Y_t - Y_{t-1}$ = change in income

This is the same system used as an example in chapter 2, except for the lagged-consumption term introduced in the consumption relationship. If we have estimated this system of equations, our first concern may be with how well this system can explain history, given values of the exogenous variables G_t and r_t over some selected period of time. Several approaches are available for solving this system at any point in time for given values of G_t, r_t, C_{t-1}, and Y_{t-1}. Typically, some variant of the Gauss-Seidel algorithm is used to solve systems of this type. This solution procedure essentially starts from a specific initial set of values for all endogenous variables and iterates through the system until all endogenous variables differ by no more than some preselected amount on two successive iterations. This is defined as a *solution point.*

To illustrate, using the simple model just presented, suppose the parameter estimates of the system were

$$C_t = 17.5 + 0.2Y_t + 0.7C_{t-1}$$

$$I_t = 100.0 - 3.0r_t + 0.2\Delta Y_t$$

Assume initial conditions, values for the period before the first solution period, say, $t = 0$, are $Y_0 = 445.0$, $C_0 = 285.0$, $I_0 = 70.0$, $G_0 = 90.0$, and $r_0 = 6.0$. Now suppose we want to solve the model for the next period, assuming that our policy variables that are exogenous to the model take on the values $G_1 = 100$ and $r_1 = 5.5$. We will accept a solution when no variable varies more than 0.05 between successive iterations.

Evaluating the consumption relationship first, the problem is that we have no value for current income. As a startup point, we might use last period's value to give us values for variables on the righthand side of our equations:

$$C_1^{(1)} = 17.5 + 0.2 * 445.0 + 0.7 * 285.0 = 306.0$$

and then for the investment relationship we could simply assign a zero starting value to ΔY_t, so

$$I_1^{(1)} = 100.0 - 3.0 * 5.5 + 0.2 * 0.0 = 83.5$$

$$Y_1^{(1)} = C_1^{(1)} + I_1^{(1)} + G_1 = 306.0 + 83.5 + 100.0 = 489.5$$

Now using the solution values for the first iteration on the righthand side of the equations, we go through the model again. In this second pass,

$$C_1^{(2)} = 17.5 + 0.2 * 489.5 + 0.7 * 285.0 = 314.9$$

$$I_1^{(2)} = 100.0 - 3.0 * 5.5 + 0.2 * (489.5 - 445.0) = 92.4$$

$$Y_1^{(2)} = 314.9 + 92.4 + 100.0 = 507.3$$

and so on, yielding the following iteration values:

	(1)	(2)	(3)	(4)	(5)	(6)	(7)	(8)
Y	489.5	507.3	514.5	517.3	518.5	518.9	519.1	519.1
C	306.0	314.9	318.5	319.0	320.5	320.7	320.8	320.8
I	83.5	92.4	96.0	97.4	98.0	98.2	98.3	98.3
G	100.0	100.0	100.0	100.0	100.0	100.0	100.0	100.0
r	5.5	5.5	5.5	5.5	5.5	5.5	5.5	5.5

In this example, none of the endogenous variables in our model, Y, C, and I, changed by more than 0.05 between the seventh and eighth iterations, and if we specify this as the unit of tolerance, we would accept the values on the eighth iteration as a solution to the model.

This, of course, is not the only algorithm for solving a model, and for the small linear model in this example, it might be as efficient to invert the matrix of coefficients to solve the model. Gauss-Seidel has been found to be very efficient, however, in solving large nonlinear systems and is now in wide use.[12] Even if the system were linear, if it were as large as most of the widely used forecasting models, it would probably be more efficient to use the Gauss-Seidel algorithm than to undertake the extensive calculations associated with large-scale matrix inversion.

Note also that in terms of computational efficiency, it is actually necessary to evaluate only a small part of the system on successive iterations. All predetermined and exogenous components need be evaluated only once. In our example on the rth iteration,

$$C_1{}^{(r)} = 0.2 * Y_1{}^{(r-1)} + (17.5 + 0.7 * 285)$$

$$I_1{}^{(r)} = 0.2 * Y_1{}^{(r-1)} + (100 - 3 * 5.5 - 0.2 * 445)$$

$$Y_1{}^{(r)} = C_1{}^{(r)} + I_1{}^{(r)} + 100$$

Additional efficiency can be achieved by shifting to the righthand side the highest iteration value for a variable or evaluating key variables more than once within a pass. Using the lagged values of endogenous variables for the first iteration reduces the number of iterations to convergence, but in general will not alter the solution value if convergence criteria are stringent enough. If, for example, we were to set $Y_1{}^{(1)} = C_1{}^{(1)} = I_1{}^{(1)} = 0$ for the first iteration, we have the path

	\multicolumn{6}{c}{Iteration}					
	1	2	3		8	9	10
Y_1	311.5	436.1	485.9	...	518.8	519.1	519.1
C_1	217.0	279.3	304.2	...	320.7	320.8	320.8
I_1	-5.5	56.8	81.7	...	98.2	98.3	98.3

We have slightly increased the number of iterations by starting the initial iterations farther from the final solution point, but we have arrived at the same final solution.

In this example, we have assumed certain values for exogenous variables, we could have as easily inserted historical values. If we have them, we could compare the results of solving the system of equations with the actual history of the economy. Suppose, for example, that the observed values for this period were $Y = 520, C = 322, I = 98, G = 100$, and $r = 5.5$. We could then calculate the error for each of the endogenous variables in the system when the system is solved simultaneously. These errors will not be the same as the errors when each equation in the system is evaluated singly. In the example, evaluation of each equation separately yields[13]

$$C = 17.5 + 0.2 * 520 + 0.7 * 285 = 321.0$$

$$I = 100.0 - 3.0 * 5.5 + 0.2 * (520 - 445) = 98.5$$

Within the sample period, the errors calculated in this latter manner will be exactly the least-squares residuals from the estimated equation, assuming that the coefficients were estimated using OLS regression methods. Beyond the sample period, we are interested in these errors as an indication of the drift in equation structure or as an indicator of serious misspecification in the equation. But in addition, we are interested in the system properties qua system. If we have satisfied ourselves that each individual equation has acceptable economic and statistical properties, there remain questions of whether the system as a whole exhibits acceptable properties. The questions here include

1. Goodness of fit of the system. How well does the system, as a system, fit historical data?
2. Stability. We are interested in whether the system will tend to dampen or amplify shocks to the economic system.
3. Multiplier effects. Given a shock to the system, what is the path that the system follows, and does it correspond to a priori information derived from economic theory?

The one-period simulation exercise where the full set of equations is solved simultaneously is a first step in evaluating goodness of fit of the system. At this point in a simulation exercise we have two options. We could continue to solve the model for the next period using actual values of both exogenous variables and lagged endogenous variables, or we could use generated solution values for the lagged endogenous variables while retaining the actual values of exogenous variables. The former option is generally referred to as a *one-period simulation* and the latter as a *dynamic simulation.* Both involve solving the model simultaneously and using the same set of exogenous variables, but in the former case, lagged variables always assume their actual historical values, while in the latter, they assume the values solved for by the model when they fall within the model solution period.

Continuing our example, if we were to solve this model for a second period, the one-period simulation would use values $Y_{t-1} = 520.0$ and $C_{t-1} = 322.0$, while the dynamic simulation would use $Y_{t-1} = 519.1$ and $C_{t-1} = 320.8$. If the model contained lags on any of the endogenous variables greater than one period, in a dynamic simulation we would continue to use historical values for the value of the lagged variable until the number of solution periods exceeded the lag period. In the first solution period, all lagged endogenous variables assume their historical values. In the second solution period, lags of length one have the values solved for in the first solution period; all variables with lags of two or more periods have historical values. In the third solution, lags of length one and two have values from the solution, while greater lags have historical values and so on. In a one-period simulation, all lags always assume historical values.

A dynamic simulation is clearly a more stringent test of a model and is clearly the exercise most like forecasting. It is a test that a model must pass before we would be willing to use it for forecasting purposes. It can be used not only to evaluate the contemporaneous relationships within a model, but also the dynamic characteristics. We are interested in both the one-period and dynamic-simulation paths because we may find that a model which exhibits satisfactory system characteristics in one-period simulations does not exhibit satisfactory system dynamics. The system may betray a tendency to follow the initial error by generating ever larger deviations in the same direction when initial conditions are not reset to historical values, or it may develop ever larger cycles. It is also possible to find that a system has acceptable dynamic characteristics for a short-period of time but has a tendency to stray from the historical path beyond that period.

The results of such simulations can be used not only to evaluate the system as to whether it offers a satisfactory explanation of history, but for large systems they are also useful diagnostic tools. If a model develops large errors when solved simultaneously and/or dynamically, it is sometimes difficult to isolate the source of the problem from full system simulations. One procedure for isolating the troublesome segments is to simulate the system by assigning exogenous values to the lefthand variable(s) generated from the suspect equation(s).[14]

If we found that our small model did not track history very well and we suspected that the investment equation was at fault, we might run a dynamic simulation in which we exogenized investment and set it equal to its historical value at each point in time. A substantial decline in system error measures would indicate that, in fact, this sector should be reevaluated.

We have referred to "acceptable" simulation properties of a system of equations without defining these characteristics. Clearly what we hope for is a system that, when solved dynamically over a historical period, will yield errors for each endogenous variable that are both small and random. We shall give particular weight to small errors at turning points—upper or lower. No single statistic will summarize either of these characteristics, and model builders and users study the error patterns of each equation in the model both for systematic and for episodic deviations from the historical path.

Summary statistics used in evaluating both simulation and forecast results include the mean square error (MSE), root mean square error, (RMSE), average absolute percentage error (AAPE), the MSE and RMSE measured in percent, number of turning-point errors, correlation or regression analysis of simulated versus actual values, Theil's inequality coefficients (U), and many other measures.[15]

The choice of error statistics and acceptable error standards is clearly a function of the use to which a model is to be put. From the viewpoint of a quarterly macroeconomic model of the United States, perhaps the most important dynamic statistics are those relating to turning-point error and measures of deviations of major macroeconomic variables from their historical paths measured by percent in the case of dollar-value variables and levels with respect to growth, inflation, and unemployment rates.

If we have performed all the simulation tests and satisfied ourselves that the model we have constructed fits the historical data, the next test is to examine the multipliers in the system. A *multiplier* is simply the change in one endogenous variable divided by a given change in an exogenous variable. While we are interested in the response characteristics of the system to most exogenous variables, the major interest of economists has been concentrated on examining the multiplier effects of government fiscal and monetary policy variables. While the numerical values that these multipliers should take are still unsettled, there are some areas of agreement on the approximate magnitude and signs of effects of certain policies, particularly in the short run. We would, for example, reject a model where the impact multiplier, the first period effect of a change, of real government purchases on GNP was negative and find suspect an American model where that impact was greater than 2.0.

In our small model, we would calculate the multiplier for government purchases by comparing two dynamic-solution paths where the only differences in exogenous variables appear in the value assumed by government purchases. Suppose we solved the model for that first period with $G_1 = 110$ rather than 100. Now the solution values are $Y_1 = 535.8$, $C_1 = 324.1$, $I_1 = 101.7$, $G_1 = 110.0$, and $r_1 = 5.5$. Evaluating the multiplier effect of real government purchases on GNP, we have

$$m_{Y.G(1)} = \frac{\Delta Y}{\Delta G} = \frac{535.8 - 519.1}{110 - 100} = 1.67$$

We could also examine the multiplier effects on consumption and investment:

$$m_{C.G(1)} = \frac{\Delta C}{\Delta G} = \frac{324.1 - 320.8}{110 - 100} = 0.33$$

$$m_{I.G(1)} = \frac{\Delta I}{\Delta G} = \frac{101.7 - 98.3}{110 - 100} = 0.34$$

That is, a $1.00 increase in government purchases increases Y by $1.67 in the first period. This is made up of the $1.00 increase in G, $0.33 extra in C, and a $0.34 increase in I. This is a dynamic model, however, and a sustained change in government purchases will have a different impact in the second period than in the first. If the original path of historical values was $r_2 = 5.5$ and $G_2 = 110.0$, then a dynamic solution for the second period would yield $Y_2 = 552.9$, $C_2 = 352.6$, and $I_2 = 90.3$. While if we continue the multiplier run with $\Delta G = 10$ ($G_2 = 120.0$), the second period solution is $Y_2 = 567.9$, $C_2 = 357.9$, and $I_2 = 90.0$.

Evaluating the second period multipliers, we find that

$$m_{Y.G(2)} = \frac{\Delta Y}{\Delta G} = \frac{567.9 - 552.9}{10} = 1.5$$

$$m_{Y.C(2)} = 0.53$$

$$m_{Y.I(2)} = -0.03$$

The dynamics of this system are such that the multiplier effect begins to decline in the second period. This is primarily caused by an actual decline in investment, partially made up by an increase in consumption.

We can continue to compare the two solution paths for our model, tracing out the dynamic-multiplier path for any of the endogenous variables. For this model, the path for the GNP multiplier is presented in figure 3-1. This multiplier path is not atypical of models with an accelerator model of investment and would not be rejected on a priori grounds.

Table 3-2 describes the complete path of the original or baseline simulation and the multiplier simulation with which we would compare it.

Validation for Forecasting

As a first step in validating a model, simulation and multiplier analysis over the sample period are necessary, but they are not sufficient to guarantee that a model will be a useful forecasting tool. While no model should be accepted if it does not pass certain criteria regarding its ability to reproduce the historical path of the economy or if it fails to generate multiplier responses akin to those suggested by economic theory and past experience, the final validation of any econometric model is its ability to produce "sensible" forecasts or, at a minimum, to be able to simulate with some degree of accuracy the path of economic phenomena outside the sample period.

While it is not unusual for postsample performance to be advocated as a criterion for model validations, the extent to which the least-squares estimation technique may obviate within sample simulation results appears to have been

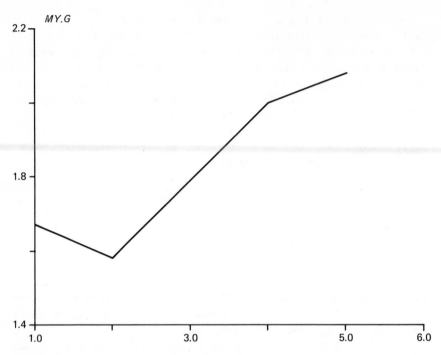

Figure 3-1. Dynamic Multiplier: Effect of Government Expenditures on GNP.

neglected. The obvious point to be made is that the least-squares estimator picks the set of single-equation estimates which minimizes

$$\sum_{t=1}^{T} (Y_t - \hat{Y}_t)^2$$

no matter what the extent of specification error. Within-sample simulations will in fact benefit from this characteristic. To choose an extreme example, one could specify a completely recursive system:

$$Y_{t1} = a_{11} + a_{21}X_{t1}$$
$$Y_{t2} = a_{12} + a_{22}X_{t2} + a_{32}Y_{t1}$$

Clearly, so long as each individual equation is chosen to have a high R^2, the system as a whole is not likely to drift far from the sample experience for within-sample simulations.

Moreover, for certain types of specification error, multiplier properties may

Table 3–2
Calculation of Dynamic Multipliers

	Original Simulation				
	Y	C	I	G	r
0	445.0	285.0	70.0	90.0	6.0
1	519.1	320.8	98.3	100.0	5.5
2	552.9	352.6	90.3	110.0	5.5
3	587.0	381.7	90.3	115.0	5.5
4	588.8	384.9	83.9	120.0	5.5
5	629.4	412.8	91.6	125.0	5.5

	Multiplier Simulation				
	Y	C	I	G	r
0	445.0	285.0	70.0	90.0	6.0
1	535.8	324.1	101.7	110.0	5.5
2	567.9	357.9	90.0	120.0	5.5
3	604.9	389.0	90.9	125.0	5.5
4	608.0	393.9	84.1	130.0	5.5
5	650.2	423.3	91.9	135.0	5.5

	Multiplier
	$m_{Y \cdot G}$
0	–
1	1.67
2	1.58
3	1.79
4	2.00
5	2.08

be approximately preserved. Suppose the correct specification of a consumer durables expenditure equation is

$$CD/Y = \beta_0 + \beta_1 P_r + \beta_2 r + \epsilon$$

or

$$CD = \beta_0 Y + \beta_1 P_r Y + \beta_2 r Y + \epsilon Y$$

where CD = expenditure on consumer durables

P_r = relative price

Y = income

r = interest rate

but the estimated equation is

$$CD = \beta_0^* + \beta_1^* P_r + \beta_2^* r + \beta_3^* Y + \epsilon^*$$

Under some fairly stringent assumptions, it is possible to show that the estimate of the marginal propensity to consume β_3^* that results from applying ordinary least squares to the misspecified equation will have statistical properties which make it likely that in the neighborhood of the means of the explanatory variables the estimated/simulated effect of an increase in Y on CD is likely to be approximately the same whichever version of the equation is estimated.[16] If the estimated marginal propensity to consume is close to the "true" value, the multiplier will also be close.

Since, in fact, the estimation technique is working so hard for us within the sample period, satisfactory reports on simulation and multiplier results over the sample period should be treated with a great deal of circumspection.

Notes

1. Much of this discussion is based on G. Fromm and G.R. Schink, "Aggregation and Econometric Models," *International Economic Review* 14, no. 1, February 1973, pp. 1-32.

2. For a detailed survey, see H.A.J. Green, *Aggregation in Economic Analysis* (Princeton, N.J.: Princeton Univ. Press, 1964).

3. For example, even if incomes are restrained by an increase in residential investment that is offset by reduced spending by government.

4. For a more formal discussion of the effects of disaggregation on forecast error, see appendix 3A.

5. See, for example, J. Kmenta, *Elements of Econometrics* (New York: Macmillan, 1971), pp. 391-405; and L.R. Klein, *A Textbook of Econometrics* (Englewood Cliffs, N.J.: Prentice-Hall, 1974), pp. 210-224.

6. See the discussion of solution procedures and the nature of a solution in the section of this chapter on "Estimation and Validation Issues for Forecasting Models."

7. J. Marschak, "Economic Measurements for Policy and Prediction," in W.C. Hood and T.C. Koopmans (eds.), *Studies in Econometric Method* (New York: Wiley, 1953).

8. See, for example, L.R. Klein, "Estimation of Interdependent Systems in Macro-Econometrics," *Econometrica* 39, 1969, pp. 171; F.M. Fisher, "Dynamic Structure and Estimation in Economy-Wide Econometric Models," in J.S. Duesenberry et al., *The Brookings Quarterly Econometric Model of the United States* (Chicago: Rand-McNally, 1965); and M.D. McCarthy, *The Wharton Quarterly Econometric Forecasting Model, Mark III* (Philadelphia: Univ. of Pennsylvania, 1972), chapter IV.

9. The justification for this approach relies on the decomposability of the covariance structure. See A. Ando and F.M. Fisher, "Near Decomposability, Partition and Aggregation, and the Relevance of Stability Discussions," *International Economic Review* 4, October 1963, pp. 53–67.

10. For an extensive discussion of the major issues, see P.J. Dhrymes et al., "Criteria for Evaluation of Econometric Models," *Annals of Economic and Social Measurement,* July 1972, pp. 291–324.

11. See P.J. Dhrymes, *Econometrics, Statistical Foundations and Applications* (New York: Harper and Row, 1970), pp. 240–277.

12. It should be noted that while no readily applied global conditions have been established for convergence of this algorithm, Gauss-Seidel has been found to be sensitive to both the ordering and normalization of equations. Additionally, while early uses of the system established convergence criteria for each variable in the system, it now appears that additional computational efficiency can be achieved by checking only a subset of the system.

13. On a single-equation basis, only stochastic equations need to be evaluated since identities should hold exactly if historical data appear on the right-hand side.

14. An example of this type of exercise can be found in A. Ando and F. Modigliani, "Econometric Analysis of Stabilization Policies," *American Economic Review* 59, no. 2, May 1969, p. 296.

15. For definitions of these statistics see chapter 5.

16. The proof of this statement is beyond the technical level of this book.

Appendix 3A
Disaggregation and
Forecast Error

Consider a forecast of Y generated either by a disaggregated system represented by equations 3.1, 3.2, and 3.3 or by a single equation such as 3.6. If we define the forecast error

$$e_{t1} = Y_{t1}^f - Y_{t1}$$

then the sample variance of the forecast error is

$$\sigma_{e_{y_1}}^2 = \sum_{t=1}^{T} (e_{t1} - \bar{e}_1)^2/T$$

where

$$\bar{e}_1 = \sum_{t=1}^{T} e_{t1}/T$$

is the mean error, and T is the number of periods for which we have observations on both forecasts and actual data.

The question of interest is whether, and under what conditions, it might be expected that disaggregation of the system would reduce either the absolute value of $\bar{e}$ and/or $\sigma_{e_{y_1}}^2$.

If equation 3.6 is used for forecasting, the errors are a result of the single-equation errors and can result from bias in parameters estimated, misspecification of the relationship, errors in initial conditions (data revision), or shocks (ϵ_{t1}^*) to the system. Also, the errors in equation 3.6 are serially correlated, and this fact may not be taken into account in forecast computations.

The same sources and possibilities for error arise in the use of the disaggregated system. However, we can now assign the sources of error to y_{t2} and y_{t3}, since

$$e_{t1} = y_{t1}^f - Y_{t1} = (Y_{t2}^f - Y_{t2}) + (Y_{t3}^f - Y_{t3}) = e_{t2} + e_{t3}$$
$$\bar{e}_1 = \bar{e}_2 + \bar{e}_3$$

and

$$\sigma_{e_{y_1}}^2 = \sum_{t=1}^{T} (e_{t1} - \bar{e}_1)^2 / T$$

$$= \sum_{t=1}^{T} [(e_{t2} - \bar{e}_2) + (e_{t3} - \bar{e}_3)]^2 / T$$

$$= \sum_{t=1}^{T} (e_{t2} - \bar{e}_2)^2 / T + \sum_{t=1}^{T} (e_{t3} - \bar{e}_3)^2 / T$$

$$+ 2 \sum_{t=1}^{T} (e_{t2} - \bar{e}_2)(e_{t3} - \bar{e}_3) / T$$

$$= \sigma_{e_{y_2}}^2 + \sigma_{e_{y_3}}^2 + 2\sigma_{e_{y_2} e_{y_3}}$$

This last term on the righthand side is the covariance of the forecast errors for y_{t2} and y_{t3}.

In terms of the mean error for forecasts of y_{t1}, the question is whether the issues discussed in chapter 3 regarding the enhancement of possibilities for more precise specification, more efficient estimation, and more precise decisions regarding policy impacts will result in the sum of errors in forecasting y_{t2} and y_{t3} being smaller than the error in forecasting y_{t1} directly.

When examining the possibility for reducing the variance of the forecast error, in addition to the question of whether the sum of the variances for y_{t2} and y_{t3} are smaller than the variance from single-equation forecasts, it is necessary to consider the covariance of the forecast errors of y_{t2} and y_{t3}. If these errors have a negative covariance, for example, if e_{t2} tends to be greater than $\bar{e}_2$ when e_{t3} is less than $\bar{e}_3$, this will enhance the possibility that disaggregation will result in smaller forecast-error variance for y_{t1} than from a more aggregated approach.

Within a disaggregated system, one might expect this type of covariance, for example, between forecasts of consumption and inventory investment. It is also possible that the mean errors for the disaggregated system might have opposite signs and a tendency to offset one another.

It should be emphasized that from an estimation point of view with accurate specification and aggregation, and with all other things being equal, we cannot generally expect this type of error reduction. The point to be made is that other things are not equal when we begin to disaggregate. We expect to reduce problems of multicollinearity, develop more precise specification, and perhaps most important from a forecasting point of view, refine our ability to monitor and analyze developments in various sectors of the economy.

4 Forecasting

The process of developing an econometric forecast occurs in two distinct phases. The initial phase is the preparation and verification of data banks and the model for forecasting. The second phase is the actual forecasting exercise involving dynamic solution of the model. It is useful to follow this breakdown in describing the mechanics of econometric forecasting.

Preparing to Forecast

The initial stages of forecast preparation are concerned with data-bank preparation and verification. Two possibilities exist. If all data within the model are available for the entire historical period, data-bank preparation simply involves preparing the available data for machine processing so that it will be available for model solution. This process itself often is not a trivial matter. Even when all the data are available, they may be on a different time frame, for example, monthly or annual when the model is quarterly. Preparation of the data will require conversion to a form consistent with the core data, which in the case of the NIPA would be quarterly at annual rates. Moreover, for the case of stock measurements, care must be taken to ensure that the appropriate measure is used to make identities consistent with respect to the point in time at which they are measured, either beginning of period, end of period, or some average. Annual data will have to be interpolated in some manner. In many cases, the interpolation process will require that data which never appear in the model be maintained to be used as interpolators. Other problems may arise if the data used in the model are not published but are transformations of published data. While much of this data processing can be mechanized, it must be continuously monitored and updated with utmost care.

The second possibility, by far the more likely for a large, disaggregated model, is that some portion of the data are not available for the most recent historical period. The Wharton quarterly model forecasting cycle follows the schedule of NIPA data releases, since this is the key data set for the model. Preliminary data on the most recently past quarter are released by the Bureau of Economic Analysis on approximately the twentieth day of the first month of the following quarter. At this point, however, data for many other important series in the model are either only partially available for the quarter or not available at all, and even the income side of the NIPA is incomplete, since neither the statistical discrepancy nor corporate profits data are included in this release.

If the missing data are exogenous variables, some method of estimating values must be developed. Among the most important series in this category in the Wharton quarterly model are data on the international economy, including quantity and price indices of world trade and price, production, and capacity-utilization information for our major trading partners. In the first month of a quarter, only partial data are available on most of these series, and for some components, data are not available for the most recent 5-month period. The historical data for these variables are prepared by examining trends in the series during the most recent period for which they are available and extending them on the basis of data which may be closely related, or a component of the data, or on the basis of recent forecasts of the data. For example, the quantity index of world trade can be extrapolated through the most recent period using a combination of information on U.S. exports, partial data on exports of industrialized countries, and information from recent forecasts of world trade.

If the missing data are endogenous variables, an alternative method of developing historical data is available. The alternative is to use model relationships which "explain" the data to extrapolate beyond the last period for which data are available. Among the data series which fall into this category in the Wharton model is information on the proportion of income taxed in various brackets which comes from the *Statistics of Income*. Sometimes as much as 3 years of history are unavailable. With the model, these data are explained by relationships of the type illustrated by table 4-1. This specification constrains the value of the dependent variable *TXOPFY*1 to lie between zero and one. The income variable and time trend account for the progressivity of the federal income tax and trend of tax exemptions and allowances not accounted for elsewhere. This is the equation for the lowest bracket, and both these effects act to reduce the proportion of taxable income taxed in this bracket as income and time increase.

To derive historical data for *TXOPFY*1, this equation is solved for the most

Table 4-1
Proportion of Income Taxed in Tax Bracket 1 = *TXOPFY*1

$$\ln \frac{TXOPFY1}{1.0 - TXOPFY1} = \underset{(-7.64076)}{-0.457568} - \underset{(-3.30468)}{0.188065} * \frac{YPTAX3\$}{NPTN16+} - \underset{(-3.32417)}{0.00916151} * DUMTIME$$

$\bar{R}^2$ = 0.995
SEE = 0.014457
DW = 2.255

Period of fit: 1964.1 to 1972.1

$YPTAX3\$$ = personal taxable income
$NPTN16+$ = noninstitutional population, age 16 and over
$DUMTIME$ = time trend 1948.1 = 1.0

Note: This equation is solved for *TXOPFY*1 for forecasting.

recent period for which data are available. The errors are examined for any systematic disturbances, and if such disturbances appear, corrections to the equation are made. Using current estimates of the explanatory variables and these corrections, the equation is used to "forecast" the historical data.[1]

For certain types of historical data, it has proved to be more reliable to use techniques similar to those used for constructing the history of exogenous variables. Chief among these are data on output originating by industrial sector in current and constant dollar terms and their associated implicit deflators. These data are actually released on an annual basis, and even when the historical data are available, quarterly numbers must be interpolated from the annual data. Generally, the current dollar output originating can be interpolated using quarterly data on income originating which are available on a quarterly basis. Output originating is the sum of income originating, capital consumption allowances, indirect business taxes, and transfers. If the latter three are a stable component of output, quarterly movements in output can be inferred from quarterly behavior of income. Since the sum of output originating by industrial sector must equal GNP, it is possible first to extrapolate current dollar output by linking the last observation of each series to the increases in income originating and then reconcile any discrepancy with total GNP. For each industry, it is then necessary to extrapolate either the implicit deflator or the constant dollar value of output originating. This is done either by using indices of production or output and/or price indices closely related to the specific industry. For example, for the implicit deflator for output of the durable manufacturing sector, extrapolation is based on the appropriate wholesale price index (WPI). For the implicit deflator for services output, extrapolation is based on the consumer price index (CPI) for services. After extrapolation, each component and the totals are checked to ensure that current dollar output is the product of the implicit deflator and constant dollar output and that the sum of output is equal to total GNP in both current and constant dollars.

After the historical data have been placed on the computer system, two further steps are taken to check the accuracy of the data and the accuracy of the model coding. The first step is to verify that all model identities are valid. This is accomplished by subtracting the righthand side of all identities from observed data on the lefthand side and verifying that the difference is zero. If, for example, the identity

$$GNP = C + I + G + NE$$

where C = consumption

$\quad I$ = investment

$\quad G$ = government purchases

$\quad NE$ = net exports

appears in the model, checking that the difference between GNP as it appears in the data bank and the sum of $C + I + G + NE$ from the data bank is zero for each period provides verification both for the data bank and model coding of that identity.

The final check on the data bank and the model is to calculate the residuals for the stochastic equations in the model on an equation-by-equation basis. This is not equivalent to solving the model because data for the righthand side of each equation come from the estimated observations in the data bank rather than from the solution.

Two types of residual checks are performed, one that includes sample-period data and one that is over the most recent period, say, the last twelve quarters, in the case of a quarterly model. In the first case, our interest is in checking that for each stochastic equation the residual observed from the model can be reconciled with the residuals from the parameter-estimation process. For example, if the equation for consumer expenditures on household operation in table 2-2 is in the model and sample period data are used to solve for $CESSUE+G$, a predicted value, then

$$r = CESSUE+G - CESSUE+G$$

should be exactly

$$e = CESSUE+G - CESSUE+G$$

where $CESSUE+G$ is the predicted value from the least-squares regression for the same period. Any discrepancy between r and e must be attributable either to an error in the data bank, a data revision, or an error in the translation of regression results to the model.[2]

After verifying that sample period residuals agree with the estimated residuals, the final validity check on the data bank is to examine residuals for the most recent period. This set of residuals should be scanned for sudden large swings beyond the normal range as an indication of data errors which might not have been captured by the identity check.

Making the Forecast

For each quarter since 1963—some 16 years—the Wharton econometric model has been put through a forecasting exercise. Out of this experience, we have developed a procedure, a methodology, for economic forecasting. Our discussion applies to the standard framework of a quarterly forecast, put in this time frame because the U.S. National Income and Product Accounts are released quarterly, but the same procedure could be adapted to a monthly model with monthly data inputs or to an annual model with yearly data updates. Indeed, the Wharton group of models includes many annual models consisting of models of the United States, Mexico, world trade, commodity markets, Brazil, New York City, and Philadelphia, and these are regularly put through a forecasting exercise.

When econometric models were first used for making forecasts (at the close of World War II in 1945), it was thought that forecasting would be straightforward. We would have a system of estimated simultaneous equations—the numerical model:

$$f_1(Y_1, Y_2, \ldots, Y_n; X_1, X_2, \ldots, X_m) = 0$$
$$\vdots$$
$$f_n(Y_1, Y_2, \ldots, Y_n; X_1, X_2, \ldots, X_m) = 0$$

where the Y's are regarded as the unknowns, and the X's are the givens. For assumed values of the X's in the forecast period, the n equation system would be solved for the n Y's, and they would constitute the forecast. This would be a dynamic process equivalent to the dynamic simulation described in chapter 3. When lagged endogenous values are present in the model, solution values appear as lags. When values of the Y's that are lagged are solved for in time period t, they are shifted to be assumed values for period $t + 1$. This procedure goes on successively from period to period. Exogenous variables must be assigned values for the X's in each forecast period, and lag values of Y's are determined step by step as the system inches forward. The procedures are those worked out for simulation exercises in the preceding chapter.

This straightforward procedure, which seems reasonable enough on the surface, treats the problem as a piece of arithmetic. There are fundamental reasons why this seemingly reasonable approach is bound to fail and cannot produce usable forecasts. There is ample evidence that it has not worked when it has been tried after the event, either as a genuine forecast or as a simulated forecast exercise.

Tests of the arithmetic approach have shown that forecasts generated from a model, estimated up to a point, and extrapolated beyond that point produced gross errors. Errors were to be expected, but those obtained would be embarrassingly large for users, either in the public or private sector. These errors would turn out to be large when compared with forecasts from simplistic rules. Such rules might be the "no-change" forecast, this period the same as the previous (observed) period, or the "same-change" forecast, this period's change from the previous period the same as the previous period's change from two periods ago. In symbols,

$$\hat{Y}_{it} = Y_{i,t-1} \qquad \text{no change}$$

or

$$\hat{Y}_{it} - Y_{i,t-1} = Y_{i,t-1} - Y_{i,t-2} \qquad \text{same change}$$

At a more sophisticated level, the pure arithmetic use of a model performs poorly in comparisons with the estimated equation:

$$Y_{it} = a_0 + a_1 Y_{i,t-1} + a_2 Y_{i,t-2} + \cdots + a_q y_{i,t-q}$$

This equation, which is a generalization of "no change" or "same change," expresses values of a given variable as a linear function of its past history. It is much more complicated than no-change or same-change models, but it is much simpler than the elaborate process of model construction. This is the autoregressive model introduced in chapter 1, and it could be extended to the more general and sophisticated autoregressive moving-average model.

While forecast errors generated by a model do not appear to be smaller than those from forecasts by the simpler methods, it should be remarked and emphasized that the lack of superiority on the part of models pertains especially to very near or short-run forecasts of one to three quarters at most. There is good evidence that forecasts from carefully constructed models stand up better over a longer time horizon of 1 full year or more than do forecasts from pure time processes, like the preceding ones, that lack structural interdependence among different parts of the economy and that fail to use exogenous variables representing policy actions.

Even the errors generated from forecasts based on purely mechanical solution of the most carefully estimated models are in many cases too large to be usable. They are also larger than forecast errors that are produced by informal judgmental methods. These latter, although subjectively varying from personal forecaster to personal forecaster, are generally more accurate in the very short run than straightforward, automatically derived forecasts from models.

What are the reasons for the apparent lack of forecasting power from carefully constructed models using the best of received macroeconomic doctrine? Within a sample period, that is, the period of data observation that underlies model construction, simulated forecast error seems to be quite small. The reasons for this were explained in the preceding chapter. But once a model is extrapolated beyond the sample period, forecast error typically enlarges rapidly.

The conceptual aspects of this problem are relatively straightforward, but some are occasionally ignored. Let us assume that we have constructed our model with tender loving care. The specification of structural relationships has a firm foundation in economic theory. The parameter estimates satisfy all theoretical priors. Error measures for historical dynamic simulations fall within acceptable bounds. Multiplier analysis results in signs and magnitudes that are plausible and satisfactory. Now we examine single-equation residuals of all variables in the model whose value is determined by a stochastic relationship. What can we expect to find? The observed errors may be attributable to

1. Normal stochastic disturbances
2. Bias in the parameter estimates
3. Misspecification, either in the stochastic or nonstochastic structure
4. Measurement errors

1. Normal stochastic disturbances. Comment hardly seems necessary except that the perception of the appropriate interpretation of residuals has sometimes failed to follow the evolution of specification. As specifications have become increasingly nonlinear, rather than concentrating analysis on the residual pattern of the estimated equation, we have chosen to examine the residuals from the level form of the relationship, say,

$$r_{it} = y_{it} - \hat{y}_{it}$$

even when the dependent variable in estimation might be $\ln y$, y/x, or Δy. Even if e_{it}, our estimation residuals, were to assume all the desirable characteristics we ascribe to it in a classical regression situation, r_{it} clearly will not under all these transformations.

2. Bias. The parameter estimates of the systems we deal with are clearly subject to simultaneous equation bias and generally may be expected to be biased as a result of incorrectly included or omitted variables and other specification errors. Thus, even in a linear system, the residuals will contain terms that are linear combinations of the independent variables in the regression and any omitted variables. In addition, we expect that the moments of any stochastic characterization of the residuals will be affected not only in their mean, but also in higher-order terms, since it is unlikely that the misspecified variables are independent of the disturbance term.[3] As noted in chapter 3, even intensive simulation analysis cannot be expected to expose many serious biases that will become evident when these results are used beyond the sample period. Recognition of these problems does not invalidate the usefulness of models either for forecasting or policy analysis. It does emphasize the necessity of using them with care.

3. Misspecification. The most important problem is clearly that of omitted variables which have a substantive impact on the dependent variable.

4. Measurement errors. We refer here not so much to the impact of measurement errors for sample-period values on parameter estimates, but to the problems of dealing with residuals based on data which are likely to be subject to substantial revision of unknown size and direction at some time in the future. Even if each of our relationships were perfectly specified and not subject to problems of bias or inconsistency, we would observe residuals in the near term

based on the difference between the actual values and reported observations of both dependent and independent variables. Economic data are always in a tentative state of observation and are regularly being revised, historically as well as contemporaneously. One possible explanation for why very simple, autoregressive models may do as well or better than large, structural models for one-period forecasts may be in the efficiency with which they process the most recent data on the state of the economy. These data are invariably very "noisy," and complex nonlinear sets of difference equations may be more greatly affected by the errors in observation.

What are we to conclude from this? Quite simply, it seems clear that given the present state of the art of model building, any attempt to mechanize the analysis of residuals and projection of these error terms for forecasting is as likely to fail as did early attempts at mechanically using the model and ignoring these errors. No simple stochastic characterization of the disturbances will encompass all the impacts just described. Judgment and intuition are critical elements in processing the information in the residuals and deciding what, if anything, should be done in terms of developing the forecast.

How to Forecast

There is a way out of the difficulty that deterioration of model performance beyond the sample period presents. It lacks the purity of the arithmetic or mechanical use of a model, yet it works and is, in our opinion, the only way to forecast the macroeconomy. The Wharton approach consists of the following steps:

1. Estimate a model over a basic sample period, redoing the model and numerical estimation every 2 or 3 years.
2. Update the data file every quarter, supplemented by within-quarter revisions of some monthly data.
3. Compute residuals from each component equation of the model over the past twelve quarters as soon as a set of new data points have been added to the computer file.
4. Specify the values of exogenous variables over the forecast horizon.
5. Study the time pattern of residuals for indicated trend or systematic bias, explaining some as a consequence of particular disturbances in the economic environment, either temporary or longer run.
6. Adjust those equations which have significant nonrandom residuals that are expected to persist, keeping these adjustment factors intact on a level or trend basis. In equations with lags of the dependent variable, the adjustment factor gets carried over from period to period in the forecast horizon. Therefore, the adjustment will not contribute a constant amount for future periods unless it is trended to wipe out the carryover effect.[4]

7. Make a preliminary forecast, and evaluate the consistency of assumptions and adjustments with the forecast solution.
8. Repeat steps 4 through 7 until exogenous assumptions and equation adjustments are consistent with the forecast.
9. Distribute this forecast to a panel of model users—as many as a few hundred—and call a meeting of users or external critics.
10. Examine the forecast with the user panel, getting their criticism of assumptions and adjustments, or getting their last-minute pieces of information about particular sectors of the economy in which they specialize.
11. Adjust the forecast based on meeting information supplied by the panel of users.
12. Revise the forecast throughout the quarter as latest data get revised or as external economic change affects the environment.
13. Return to step 1 and repeat these steps as the next quarterly round.

The administration of an econometric forecast is an important aspect of the whole process. There must be a regularly maintained data file, a method for quickly adding to this file, for revising it where needed, and for accessing it through computer-based software that can be automated for dynamic solution or simulation in a forecast mode. The electronic computer has been harnessed effectively for this phase of operations. Within 48 or 72 hours, a data file of some thousands of economic series can be made ready for use in steps 2 through 6. The update procedures and the model-solution procedures are very fast once the new information of each forecast round has been digested and entered.

We have already discussed various aspects of steps 1 through 3. The important thing is to explain how assumptions and adjustments are made and how a forecast meeting is conducted in order to implement a feedback process from the user panel of field experts to the model operators. The rest of this chapter is concerned with those steps (4 through 12) which produce a typical Wharton forecast.

Steps 4 through 6 absorb a significant amount of the resources that go into producing a forecast. Some notion of the magnitude of the task can be gained by recognizing that a decision must be made regarding the values that each exogenous variable will assume and the value of any correction to each stochastic equation for each forecast period. For a typical quarterly forecast, this involves the specification of nearly 10,000 pieces of data.

Step 4. Exogenous Assumptions

The values assigned to exogenous variables have a dramatic impact on the solution. Great care must be taken in their calculation to ensure consistency across assumptions and to facilitate the explanation and modification of the assumptions. Certain of the exogenous variables can be specified for the forecast on a mechanical basis. These include seasonal dummies, time trends, and other variables which have no behavioral basis. Other variables require a substantial amount of analysis. Table 4-2 details the analysis that underlies specification of a single exogenous variable, the value of U.S. imports of petroleum. To arrive at a value for this exogenous variable, the forecasting group specifies total domestic demand for crude and refined products, inventory accumulation, the components of domestic supply, and imports in millions of barrels per day. An assumption is then made concerning the average import price. The cost of these imports is derived from the import and price numbers. The obvious question is why engage in these extraneous calculations when ultimately only the value of imports is necessary for solving the model? Indeed, until quite recently we simply derived a total number on the basis of trends and consultation with industry specialists within the Wharton membership. The additional detail for this assumption was developed in response to increased interest in the energy sector and to facilitate analysis of the impact on the U.S. economy of both OPEC prices and domestic energy policies. The detailed analysis of petroleum imports allows users to modify quickly the underlying assumptions concerning demand, supply, imports, or pricing to alter the value of imports. The calculations in table 4-2 were made for a forecast preceding the OPEC decision (December 1977) to hold world oil prices at existing levels for the next several months. As soon as this information became available, these calculations were done again with an altered assumption for average import price per barrel. In addition, the breakdown of domestic production here is carried over to analysis of modifications necessary to analyze different sets of price-control and tax policies. For example, the impact of the imposition of the well-head equalization tax proposed by the administration in 1977 would have varied depending on the composition of production, since the tax would have appeared in stages keyed to the various

Table 4-2
Petroleum Demand/Supply Assumptions

	1977.4	1978.1	1978.2	1978.3
U.S. total crude and product demand (MBD)	17.5	18.3	19.1	19.3
Domestic inventory accumulation (MBD)	1.3	1.1	0.5	0.6
Domestic crude and product output (MBD)	10.3	10.7	10.8	10.9
Total domestic crude production (MBD)	8.2	8.6	8.7	8.8
Base domestic crude production (MBD)	7.8	7.8	7.7	7.6
Alaskan production (MBD)	0.4	0.8	1.0	1.2
Outer continental shelf production (MBD)	0.0	0.0	0.0	0.0
Crude and product imports (MBD)	8.5	8.7	8.8	9.0
Average import price per barrel	14.39	14.53	15.26	15.52
Annualized cost of fuel imports (billions $)	44.0	45.5	48.3	50.3

price-control levels attached to new, old, and stripper oil. By specifying these components together with the total, it is possible to ensure that assumptions are consistent across the entire set of exogenous variables affected by developments in the petroleum industry. Moreover, it ensures that if a user desires to modify these assumptions, for example, with respect to how quickly production in Alaska rises, he can trace that assumption through the set of variables affected. A final advantage for the great detail displayed in calculating these variables is that it enables the user to examine and discuss possible disagreements with the assumptions in terms of their components rather than trying to grapple with an aggregate number.

The problem of developing assumptions for the energy sector illustrates the interplay between the private sector and government policy in making assumptions about exogenous variables. While domestic production is largely a function of private-sector decisions, the demand side must be evaluated with a consideration for pricing policies and government decisions on inventories. Most important among the exogenous variables for forecasting, however, may be the set of public-sector variables listed in chapter 2. For establishing values for these variables, the forecaster must become a political economist.

To illustrate the types of problems involved here, consider the difficulty in specifying forecast values for a single component of the federal budget, grants-in-aid. During the early months of 1977, the administration was proposing a budget for FY78 which included $81.2 billion for this category. A substantial proportion of this was to be part of a stimulus package aimed at generating increased expenditures at the state and local government level. At the same time, bills were moving through Congress which included substantially greater stimulus and would have implied a FY78 total of $85.3 billion for grants-in-aid. In addition to choosing between these two totals, or modifying them and using still a third number, the forecaster must evaluate the impact of the incremental grants on state and local purchases of goods and services, which is also exogenous. Studies have indicated that some portion of increased grants will be spent, but it is also clear that some will be used to alleviate the state and local tax burden and some simply result in a greater surplus or lower deficit in the state and local sector. An additional complication is that the type of grant made can affect the state and local sector not only when it is made, but also into the future. This is particularly true when the grant is tied to capital expenditures, as in the case of the Local Public Works Employment Act of 1976. This type of grant will not only increase capital expenditures in the near term, but also is likely to reduce them at some time in the future by causing a shifting in the timing of capital expenditure without substantially increasing the desired capital stock. Each of these factors must be considered in terms of political influences, economic positions, and bureaucratic capabilities as the assumptions are detailed.

Steps 5 and 6. Residuals and Endogenous Equation Adjustment

Even while these assumptions are being constructed, the last set of residuals which were checked to verify the data bank and model—those for the stochastic equations over recent history—are being studied for information relevant for forecasting.[5] Each forecast begins with an examination of single-equation residuals over the most recent historical period. For the quarterly model, this starts with an examination of the last thirteen quarters. This means that the residuals being considered are almost universally beyond the sample period. These errors are studied with the intent of developing a projection of the values they will assume during the forecast period. These projected values are then added to the relevant variables. If, for example, the projected vector of residuals is $\hat{e}_t$ and the relationship to which they will be attached is $y_t = a_0 + a_1 X_t$ then the forecast for y_t is calculated as

$$y_t = a_0 + a_1 X_t + \hat{e}_t$$

the vector, $\hat{e}_t$, of projected residuals, is called a constant term adjustment or con adjustment. This terminology derives from the observation that for linear relationships, this practice is equivalent to shifting the intercept or constant term of the equation.

A slight digression is merited here to point out that it is indeed the single-equation errors and not full-system errors which are of interest. Given the type of systems with which we are concerned, observed errors, in any one equation or set of equations from a system solution, cannot easily be assigned to a single set of equations. Given the interdependence of the system, developing adjustments to correct such errors is generally a nontrivial problem. The simple example of the generally highly interdependent nature of the wage and price sectors should make the problem clear. If, in a system solution, wages and prices are observed to err in the same direction, which is to be adjusted and by how much (given that the partial derivative of each, with respect to the other, is positive)? Single-equation residuals allow one to examine the error each relationship makes when the rest of the system assumes the observed values. Moreover, while no proof that a unique global solution exists for the nonlinear systems when the Gauss-Seidel method is used to solve them, it appears to be true that if single-equation residuals are added to each stochastic relationship, the system will duplicate its historical path. We infer from this that the appropriate goal for the forecast is to project single-equation errors.

The objective in examining residuals is (1) to detect nonzero means in the residuals, (2) nonrandom patterns in the residuals, and (3) outliers which may be attributable to either mechanical errors in creating the data bank or explicable in terms of special events.

The goal is clear. If in fact residuals exhibit any pattern other than that of randomly distributed variables with zero means, constant variance, and temporal independence, our forecast is likely to be improved by recognizing this.[6] It is also true that in any case where a lagged dependent variable or autoregressive disturbance appears in a relationship, one may want to offset the impact of explicable outliers in the subsequent period.

The considerations involved in initial adjustments of constant terms of individual equations for a forecast are most easily introduced by example. The examples are all drawn from the forecast prepared for the May 30, 1978 release. This means that the initial examination of residuals is based on the period from 197501 to 197801. This period begins with the trough quarter of the 1974 recession and so contains data only on the recovery phase of the cycle. The last quarter in this period is one in which, at the time the forecast was being prepared, constant dollar GNP was estimated to have declined at an annual rate of 0.4%. The explanation for the decline is largely based on unusually severe weather conditions which covered large sections of the United States and a coal miners' strike which began late in December and was not ended until the beginning of the second quarter. These events become relevant to the adjustments developed for the forecast.

Table 4-3 contains selected entries for the residual calculations in May 1978 after the 45-day NIPA data (i.e., first revision of the preliminary data—15-day NIPA data) were released. These illustrate a range of problems for adjustment decisions.

The first set of data is concerned with determination of currency in the hands of the public $FCU\$$. As indicated, during this thirteen-quarter period, the currency relationship was subject to disturbances which appear to have no strong trend and a mean of $0.4 billion, amounting to something less than 0.5%, on average, of the actual value of $FCU\$$. The adjustment to the constant term of the currency equation was set equal to 0.4 for each of the forecast periods. While this seems straightforward, the formulation of the equation occasionally raises some questions which should be addressed. The estimated form of this equation is log-linear with a lagged dependent variable. In the simplest context, say, for example, of the form

$$\ln y_t = \alpha + \beta \ln y_{t-1} + \epsilon_t \tag{4.1}$$

while the model solution form is

$$y_t = \exp\left(a + b \ln y_{t-1}\right) + CON_t \tag{4.2}$$

where CON_t represents the adjustment to the equation for forecasting period t. The residual that is examined in preparing to forecast is

$$r_t = y_t - \exp\left(a + b \ln y_{t-1}\right) \tag{4.3}$$

Table 4-3
Residuals for Forecast, May, 1978

FCU$ — Currency in Circulation (in the hands of the public)

Additive Adjustments	197501	197502	197503	197504	197601	197602	197603	197604	197701	197702	197703	197704	197801
Actual	68.833	70.200	71.700	73.200	75.067	77.200	78.600	80.233	81.867	83.700	85.633	87.767	89.967
Predicted	68.818	70.517	72.002	73.606	75.234	77.115	79.248	80.826	82.586	84.249	86.120	88.212	90.336
Residual	0.015	-0.317	-0.302	-0.406	-0.167	0.085	-0.648	-0.593	-0.720	-0.549	-0.487	-0.445	-0.369

FRMCP4M — Interest Rate, 4-6-Month Prime Commercial Paper

Additive Adjustments	197501	197502	197503	197504	197601	197602	197603	197604	197701	197702	197703	197704	197801
Actual	6.563	5.920	6.667	6.120	5.290	5.570	5.530	4.990	4.810	5.237	5.807	6.593	6.797
Predicted	9.377	8.290	8.240	9.059	8.615	9.434	10.654	11.942	12.058	12.175	12.757	13.127	13.720
Residual	-2.813	-2.370	-1.573	-2.939	-3.325	-3.864	-5.124	-6.952	-7.248	-6.938	-6.950	-6.534	-6.924

CEDO — Personal Consumption Expenditures, Durable Goods, Other Durables

Additive Adjustments	197501	197502	197503	197504	197601	197602	197603	197604	197701	197702	197703	197704	197801
Actual	17.200	17.600	18.100	18.500	18.700	18.700	19.000	19.500	19.400	19.800	20.200	21.600	20.800
Predicted	16.798	18.017	17.661	18.505	18.861	18.970	18.923	18.305	19.893	20.043	20.229	20.760	20.871
Residual	0.402	-0.417	0.439	-0.005	-0.161	-0.270	0.077	0.195	-0.493	-0.243	-0.029	0.840	-1.071

IA2RGT — Investments Anticipated, New Plant and Equipment, Transportation, Two Quarters Ahead

Additive Adjustments	197501	197502	197503	197504	197601	197602	197603	197604	197701	197702	197703	197704	197801
Actual	5.445	5.941	5.666	4.996	5.037	4.625	4.871	4.315	4.449	4.557	4.588	4.637	5.245
Predicted	8.527	7.047	6.068	5.851	6.465	6.714	6.516	7.110	7.164	6.866	6.915	7.270	7.521
Residual	-3.071	-1.106	-0.402	-0.855	-1.428	-2.062	-1.645	-2.795	-2.715	-2.309	-2.327	-2.633	-2.276

IARGC48 — Investment, New Plant and Equipment, Communications

Additive Adjustments	197501	197502	197503	197504	197601	197602	197603	197604	197701	197702	197703	197704	197801
Actual	10.397	9.948	9.693	9.018	9.167	9.158	9.799	10.149	9.958	10.609	11.164	10.540	10.909
Predicted	12.868	12.857	12.759	12.868	13.065	13.435	13.873	14.640	15.380	15.817	16.949	17.783	17.946
Residual	-2.471	-3.372	-3.066	-3.849	-3.899	-4.277	-4.074	-4.491	-5.430	-5.207	-5.785	-7.243	-7.037

PWPC* — Wholesale Price Index, by Processing, Crude Materials

Additive Adjustments	197501	197502	197503	197504	197601	197602	197603	197604	197701	197702	197703	197704	197801
Actual	185.833	194.400	204.867	202.633	199.667	207.067	208.133	205.500	214.500	221.967	209.467	211.233	225.267
Predicted	221.537	227.944	238.344	232.251	234.508	241.976	239.267	225.340	238.101	244.632	231.864	233.525	249.303
Residual	-35.704	-33.544	-33.478	-29.617	-34.841	-34.910	-31.134	-19.840	-23.601	-22.666	-22.397	-22.292	-24.037

KIBINOTT — Inventory Stock, Nonfarm, Other

Additive Adjustments	197501	197502	197503	197504	197601	197602	197603	197604	197701	197702	197703	197704	197801
Actual	23.900	23.300	23.300	23.400	23.500	23.500	23.400	23.600	23.500	23.600	23.700	23.800	23.400
Predicted	24.356	23.859	23.555	23.632	23.745	23.860	23.799	23.694	23.968	23.850	23.813	23.964	24.115
Residual	-0.456	-0.559	-0.255	-0.232	-0.245	-0.360	-0.399	-0.094	-0.468	-0.250	-0.113	-0.164	-0.715

HSPRS1 — Housing Starts, Private (Including Farm), One-Unit Structures

Additive Adjustments	197501	197502	197503	197504	197601	197602	197603	197604	197701	197702	197703	197704	197801
Actual	0.734	0.848	0.950	1.033	1.093	1.107	1.184	1.264	1.287	1.436	1.472	1.550	1.234
Predicted	0.460	0.464	0.539	0.663	0.802	0.928	0.987	0.977	0.972	0.997	0.978	0.946	0.905
Residual	0.273	0.384	0.411	0.370	0.291	0.179	0.197	0.287	0.315	0.439	0.494	0.604	0.329

SAWRRDAV — Sales, Retail, New Passenger Cars, Domestic plus Imports

Additive Adjustments	197501	197502	197503	197504	197601	197602	197603	197604	197701	197702	197703	197704	197801
Actual	8.333	7.933	9.033	9.400	10.133	10.133	9.867	10.233	11.233	11.667	10.967	10.967	10.733
Predicted	9.979	10.012	9.754	9.690	9.704	9.880	9.924	9.917	9.996	10.140	10.265	10.462	10.522
Residual	-1.645	-2.079	-0.720	-0.290	0.430	0.253	-0.057	0.316	1.237	1.526	0.702	0.505	0.211

which is related to the residual from the estimated equation e_t by

$$r_t = [\exp (a + b \ln y_{t-1})] \; [\exp (e_t) - 1] \tag{4.4}$$

While r_t is clearly going to have different properties than e_t, it remains true that a "good" forecast for r_t, in the sense of being "close" to the error in equation 4.4, which is used to forecast with equation 4.2, will result in forecasts for y_t that are essentially the same as a "good" forecast of e_t, which is then transformed by equation 4.4 or used directly in equation 4.1.[7] The relevant issue, then, is not on which residual or form of the relationship adjustments are developed, but the accuracy with which the projections replicate the behavior of disturbances. The adjustment for the next equation presents a different set of problems. This is the basic money-demand equation in the model which in solution is renormalized to determine the short-term interest rate *FRMCP4M*. As have almost all money-demand relationships estimated with a sample period that ended in 1974, this relationship has developed sizable errors in the post-sample period.[8] There is also a substantial trend in the errors during this period. While the mean error is -5.1, the mean for the four quarters of 1975 is -2.4; for 1976, -4.8; and for 1977, -6.9. This occurred despite a difference in the average rate for 1975 and 1977 of only 0.7. While any regression fit to these data on residuals would undoubtedly not reject the hypothesis of first-order serial correlation, also observe that for the last five quarters the residual has had a mean of -6.92 with a standard deviation of less than 0.25. Based on the judgment that these last five periods were likely to be more representative of the future than the earlier period, the initial adjustment for this relationship was set at -6.9 for each period. This is clearly substantially different from a mechanical projection based on means or from some form of regression analysis. During the forecast, modifications were made to this projection.

The residual pattern for *CEDO,* consumer expenditures on durables other than autos and parts and household durables, presents still another aspect of the problem of projecting disturbances. The mean error for the thirteen-quarter period is -0.06. However, the two largest errors, in absolute value almost twice the size of the next largest, occur in the two most recent periods for which observations are available. Moreover, these two errors are of opposite signs, with 197704 underpredicted and 197801 overpredicted. The mean error for the first eleven periods is -0.05, with a standard deviation of 0.3. Including the two most recent periods changes the mean only marginally but increases the standard deviation by 60.0%, to near 0.5. Given the sharp slowing of income growth as a result of the coal miners' strike and bad weather in the first quarter, there was some reason to expect that 197801 might be a temporary aberration caused by an inability of the equation to pick up this sharp short swing. This hypothesis does not explain the fourth-quarter underprediction. Additional considerations are the greater possibility of measurement error in these very recent data. On the basis of these considerations and with no discernible strong trend, the constant adjustment was set at a flat value of -0.05.

Analysis of the residuals in these first three equations resulted in projections of flat constant adjustments; and analysis of errors in the next three equations results in trend projections for these disturbances.

The first relationship is the projection for investment anticipations of the transportation industry.[9] The mean error for the period is -1.97. For the last four periods, the mean is -2.39. From mid-1975 through late 1976, there is a discernible trend, and beyond that period, errors have oscillated about approximately -2.5. We also had reason to suspect that one of the major explanatory variables, output originating in transportation, was understated in the data available for 1977, resulting in a low projection for investment. With this in mind, the original projection for this adjustment was based on a trend, but one somewhat lower than that from this period.[10] The trend increment from 197502 to 197801 was -0.12 per period. Our initial adjustment was -2.30 for the initial forecast period, with an increment of -0.07 in each period.

A stronger trend appears in the errors in the equation for $IARGC48$, investment by the communications industry. A linear regression fit to the residuals in table 4-3 results in

$$\hat{e} = -2.13 - 0.36TIME \qquad R^2 = 0.92$$

Again, however, we expect that the unusual disturbances in our endpoint may have affected the equation in a manner which results in a smaller error than would normally have occurred. Our initial projection of this disturbance was -7.4 in the first period, with increments of -0.5 in each successive period.

The movement in the residuals for the crude materials price index $PWPC^*$ are not as easily explained by a time trend. Here a regression on these observations yields

$$\hat{e} = -37.1 + 1.3TIME \qquad R^2 = 0.7$$

If this thirteen-quarter period is divided into two segments, 197001-197603 and 197604-197801, rather than a trend in errors, there appears to be a shift. The first has a mean of -33.3 with a standard deviation of 2.2, the second has a mean of -22.5 and a standard deviation of 1.5. Two considerations entered the determination of the adjustment used for this relationship. First, we observed that there is a substantial difference in growth rates for the dependent variable during these two periods, an annual rate of increase of 22% in the first period versus 15% in the second. In addition, we feel strongly that this equation is misspecified[11] and that the misspecification results in a failure to account for world commodity prices in sufficient detail. This is reflected in the greater overestimates in 1975 when world commodity prices declined precipitously and in smaller errors during the latter period as commodity prices rose. Our expectation, in part based on earlier forecasting rounds, was that the world recovery would continue at a moderate pace through the forecast period, that, as a result, commodity prices would continue to rise, and that the absolute value of the error of this relationship would continue to decline. The adjustment to this relationship was set at an initial value of −23.0 and incremented by 1.0 each period.

The final three sets of residuals in table 4-3 involve a mixture of the type of adjustment based on residual analysis and that based on specific disturbances. They are included here because the final adjustment is based on residual analysis and the specific disturbance impact estimate is, in part, based on residual analysis.

The variable *KIBINOTT* measures the stock of nonfarm, nonmanufacturing, nontrade inventories. The stock value has been overestimated in every period observed, with an average error of −0.33 and a standard deviation of 0.18. The final period error lies more than two standard deviations from the mean based on all thirteen periods and, on the basis of the first twelve periods, nearly three standard deviations from the mean. It was our judgment that a great deal of this overestimation in inventories was explained by the strike and weather patterns in the first quarter. Utility inventories of coal and pipeline holdings of natural gas both appear in this category. The rundown of these inventories resulting from the strike and weather were unlikely to be fully captured by this relationship, where the major explanatory variable is consumer expenditures. Given the settlement of the strike near the end of the first quarter, it was also our expectation that the equation would not pick up the inventory rebuilding following the strike. A combination of external information and residual analysis led us to conclude that something near 0.6 of the 0.7 overestimate in the fourth quarter was attributable to the strike rundown. Sources within the utilities industry also felt that with some delay in bringing the mines back up to normal production levels and expected high levels of economic activity in the second quarter followed by summer demands on electric utilities' inventories, stocks in this sector were likely to remain below normal levels until at least the end of the year.

Based on the residual pattern, we projected the normal disturbance for this relationship at a value of −0.25. Calculation of the adjustment for the additional accumulation was complicated by the existence of an autoregressive correction factor of 0.985.[12] If our supposition concerning the size of the effects is correct, the autoregressive correction will depress the estimated stock by 0.6 in the first period because of the fourth-period error. To offset this completely, we would add 0.6 to the base value of −0.25. We also have information, as noted earlier, that leads us to believe that the increment in stocks will stay somewhat below normal levels in the second quarter. We therefore subtracted an additional 0.05 to yield an adjustment of 0.3. No allowance for stock recovery is made in this calculation, and the rebuilding is assumed to be spread over the next five quarters. After allowance for the autoregressive correction, the final adjustments for the first eight quarters of the forecast were 0.3, 0.48, 0.2, 0.0, -0.1, -0.2, -0.25, and -0.25.

Similar issues arise in the relationships for private single-family housing starts *HSPRS*1. The appropriate adjustment in this relationship, however, is complicated by a less distinct pattern in the residuals. Superficially, the residual for the last quarter does not appear to have been affected by anything greatly different from the process generating the residuals in the preceding twelve quarters. If, however, attention is concentrated on the period 197602-197704, a break in the residual pattern becomes apparent. During this period, a strong trend is present, with the equation errors rising steadily from 0.18 to 0.60. If this trend had been extrapolated into 197801, we would have seen actual starts in the vicinity of 1.5 to 1.6. It is generally accepted that some of the decline in housing starts in the first quarter of 1978 is attributable to weather conditions. It is also true, however, that mortgage markets came under some pressure in this quarter from rising rates and reduced inflows to financial intermediaries, and some of the decline may be due to this. Starts that were held up by weather conditions will be made up largely in the second and third quarters, and this should be reflected in the adjustment. The problems are how to estimate these and what to do with the adjustments beyond that quarter. Despite the trend on which the estimate for weather-reduced starts is based, the base adjustment for starts was projected at 0.4. This is below the mean residual for the last four quarters but above that for the preceding nine quarters. The selection of a level adjustment was based on the judgment that any trend in future errors would be determined by whether starts were rising or falling, and we did not want to prejudge this. After allowance for weather-reduced starts, the constant adjustments were 0.68 in 197802, 0.55 in 197803, and 0.4 thereafter.

The final example is the relationship for projecting unit sales of automobiles. The residual pattern indicates a failure of the equation to capture the cycle in auto sales. The relationship failed to predict any of the six turning points over the period examined. Moreover, during this period the residuals changed from an average error of -1.2 in 1975 to 0.235 in 1976 and 0.993 in 1977. While the first-quarter residual was small relative to the errors from the preceding year, it was also true that auto sales during the January-February period were very slow but had picked up strongly during March. Based on data for April and early May that were available while the forecast was in preparation, it seemed clear that the second-quarter value for *SAWRRDAV* was going to be 11.5 or more. After allowing for the impact of cold weather and the coal strike on the first-quarter error and considering errors for the last year, it was decided to project the adjustment at a level of 0.75.

From these examples, it is clear that a great deal of judgment is involved in these adjustments. In addition to the pattern of the errors themselves, information on specification, possible measurement errors, and general and specific economic events are brought into the analysis. To this point, the only instances where judgments about the future evolution of the economy impinged on our decisions was in the constant adjustment for *PWPC**, where consideration of the future behavior of world commodity prices, exogenous to the model, influenced our decision and where industry information on specific inventory patterns affected *KIBINOTT*.

As might be inferred from the discussion, these initial adjustments are reviewed and may be modified in the course of finalizing the forecast. Before discussing this practice and the analysis on which it is based, it is useful to briefly survey an altogether different source of adjustments based on episodic occurrences of which we have, or assume we have, foreknowledge.

Quite often we find it necessary to include in our forecast assumptions about future events which cannot adequately be captured by the present model structure through exogenous variable changes. Obvious examples include introduction of a tax credit to replace the current exemption and the impact of refunds and credits from energy taxes on investment patterns. Innovations in policy with no sample experience on which to base parameter estimates will necessitate judgmental evaluation of impacts for any model. Invariably, there will also be a substantial number of events on the horizon which must be handled by adjustment terms because the current model structure cannot capture the expected impacts. Examples here could include issues such as the proposal to apply different wage ceilings to employer and employee contributions to Social Security. Clearly these could have been treated separately in the past, but since over the sample period rates and ceilings had been the same for both groups, a single relationship explained total contributions. Our initial attempts to examine this proposal required that we select one ceiling and one rate and adjust the equation to account for this change.

Additional sources for this type of adjustment arise from differences between average and marginal effects of exogenous variables. For example, as a result of current legislation, agricultural subsidies will rise in 1978 and 1979. Only total subsidies less surpluses appear in the model, and if this exogenous variable is increased and no other changes are made to the model input stream, the major impact is an increase in corporate profits. To achieve the proper impact on the income side, farm proprietors' incomes must be corrected with an adjustment. A similar consideration arises in connection with the output impact of an increase in federal government purchases. A marginal increase attributable to purchases of the Commodity Credit Corporation should not result in the average impact of an increase in federal nondefense purchases, but should result in an increase in agricultural output. Again, adjustments are used to correct model responses based on average relationships.

Table 4-4 documents two of these calculations from recent forecasts. The top half of the table contains the detail of the calculations for the adjustment to federal personal income tax collections. The base adjustment was developed

Table 4-4
Adjustments to Tax and Farm Income Equations

	78.2	78.3	78.4	79.1	79.2	79.3	79.4	80.1
Federal government personal taxes (*TXCPF*$)								
Base adjustment	-4.0	-4.0	-4.0	-4.0	-4.0	-4.0	-4.0	-4.0
Decrease due to adoption of personal tax credit	0.0	0.0	0.0	-25.9	-26.0	-26.0	-25.9	-25.9
Increase due to proposed tax reform	0.0	0.0	0.0	7.0	7.0	7.0	7.0	7.3
Refund for standard deduction change	-4.2	0.0	0.0	0.0	0.0	0.0	0.0	0.0
Residential energy conservation credit	0.0	0.0	0.0	-0.2	-0.2	0.0	0.0	-0.25
Total	-8.2	-4.0	-4.0	-23.1	-23.2	-23.0	-22.9	-22.85
Farm proprietors income (*YENTF*$)								
Base adjustment	-1.5	-1.5	-1.5	-1.5	-1.5	-1.5	-1.5	-1.5
Increase due to subsidies	1.6	0.2	2.1	-1.0	-0.2	0.2	2.1	-1.0
Total	0.1	-1.3	0.6	-2.5	-1.7	-1.3	0.6	-2.5

by residual analysis. It is relevant to any projection based on tax legislation currently in force. In addition to this base adjustment, allowance is made in the adjustment for four separate legislative changes.

The first two lines relate to the tax cut projected for 1979. This was basically assumed to be a scaled-down version of the original proposal made by the administration. Rates were changed (not proportionately across brackets), the personal exemption was eliminated, a personal tax credit replaced the exemption, and certain "reforms" were instituted which result in increased collections. In the original administration proposal, the credit was $240 per capita. Then the administration and congressional leaders apparently agreed on a lower tax cut than originally requested, without discussing specific revision. The credit was reduced to capture this effect. The effects are based on the assumption that deductions for state and local government taxes and medical and casualty deductions will be eliminated. The third line reflects a change in the standard deduction provisions of the income tax in 1977 which was not reflected in withholding schedules and was expected to result in lower collections in the first and second quarter of 1978. Finally, the last line was based on calculations concerning the estimated value of tax credits for residential investment in energy conservation which were expected to be part of energy legislation.

Clearly, the detail of these calculations is irrelevant for the solution of the model. Only a total is needed for each equation, but components of the tax adjustments are important for the forecasters' housekeeping and for conveying to other model users information relevant for constructing alternative scenarios.

The lower half of the table contains the detail of calculations used to adjust farm proprietors' income to reflect the expected impact of the farm subsidy program. In building up our assumptions for federal subsidies less surpluses, we made an allowance for subsidies under the 1977 farm program, which were 1.6, 1.6, 3.5, 2.1, 1.6, 1.6, 3.5, and 2.1 for the first eight quarters of the forecast.[13] The calculation of the adjustment necessary to increase $YENTF\$$ by this amount is complicated by the specification of the equation which takes the form

$$YENTF\$/(XAG\$ - WBCAG\$) = \alpha_0 + \alpha_1(PFPC*/PFR*) + \rho U_{t-1}$$

where $XAG\$$ = output originating in agriculture

   $WBCAG\$$ = compensation in agriculture

     $PFPC*$ = index of prices received by farmers

      $PFR*$ = index of prices received by farmers

     ρU_{t-1} = autoregressive disturbance

While the adjustment to the level of $YENTF\$$ for the first period requires only that we add the desired amount, the second-period calculation must net out the value for

$$\rho CON*(XAG\$ - WBCAG\$)/(XAG\$ - WBCAG\$)_{-1}$$

As an initial estimate for this value, and for ease of calculation, this final ratio was assumed to be 1.0 over the forecast horizon, resulting in the calculation shown here.

Steps 7 and 8. Forecasting and Consistency Evaluation

After specifying values for each exogenous variable, each lag in the initial period, and each adjustment term, we are prepared actually to solve the model over the forecast period. This initial solution must be carefully examined for a variety of possible errors. The most obvious is to ensure that any human error has been eliminated in placing our assumptions and adjustments in the model solution program. After eliminating these, however, the most complex aspect of forecasting begins. The forecaster must now carefully evaluate the consistency of his forecast solution with his assumptions.

The solution must be examined for answers to the following types of questions:

Are the assumptions for exchange rates (exogenous) consistent with the solution for the trade balance?

Is the solution for interest rates and/or monetary stocks likely to bring about a monetary policy different from the assumed policy?

Is the path of the economy in this solution likely to alter fiscal policy from that assumed?

Is the overall inflation rate in the solution consistent with inflation rates in exogenous prices?

Given this path for the U.S. economy, are the assumptions for the economies of our major trading partners the most likely paths for them to follow?

In addition to these questions regarding consistency, the solution must be examined for distortions that might have been introduced in the interrelationships among endogenous variables through adjustments made to the model:

Have adjustments to the consumption equations distorted the savings/income relationship?

Are the relationships among prices, wages, and productivity satisfactory?

Do the relationships among employment, manhours, and the average work week follow a normal cyclical pattern?

Is the distribution of consumer expenditures among categories of final demand and the distribution of income consistent with the evolution of prices, wages and interest rates.

Has the distribution of output followed a sensible pattern?

The list of internal consistency checks can be extended to great length. The final questions are whether the forecast line by line agrees with the intuitions and knowledge of the forecaster, and if not, is there a structural explanation for the counterintuitive result?

In a large, highly simultaneous system, this procedure can take on the characteristics of some of the more obscure inferential processes of Sherlock Holmes. In many cases, the source of difficulties can be identified only after examination of the entire forecast. Again, an example is useful for illustrating the type of analysis which occurs.

As discussed earlier, the initial adjustment for unit sales of automobiles was set at 0.75. Two aspects of the initial projection for this variable were disturbing. The first was that the projection for the second-quarter value of *SAWRRDAV* was 11.1 when information on sales for the first 6 weeks of the quarter indicated a likely value near 11.5 to 11.7 for the quarter. The second disturbing result from this initial run was a projection for a strong increase in automobile sales in 1979 and 1980, during a period when growth in constant dollar personal disposable income was expected to slow.

The first part of this problem resulted in an increase in the constant adjustment of 0.35 in 197802 and 0.1 in 197803. These adjustments were made on the judgment that the deviation in the residual pattern observed in the fourth quarter was partially attributable to the effects of weather and the coal strike. These sales were assumed to have simply been delayed and were expected to be made up in the second and third quarters of 1978. The residual adjustment reflects this expectation.

Given the pattern of past errors, there is some question concerning the cyclical behavior of future residuals. With the observed pattern of sales, the apparent anomaly may be attributed to the flat constant adjustment. Further investigation, however, revealed that during the initial forecast, a sharp drop in the relative price of automobiles occurred, which was eventually traced to the adjustment in the automobile price equation which had been projected at a level based on the average error over the last thirteen quarters. Based on the increase in the forecast in this price relative to other prices, a reexamination of the residual pattern indicated a strong possibility of a break in the error pattern, with higher errors possible in the future.

Similar stories may be developed about other adjustments in the model. The essence of a description of the modifications to adjustments that occur during this process is that at each stage a modification to any equation must satisfy the criteria that it be based on and be consistent with information currently available either in terms of residuals, current information, such as the auto sales data, or the assumptions about the behavior of exogenous variables. In addition, we impose the general criteria that, unless compelling internal consistency requires some alternative, adjustments will be either flat or trended, and that exceptions to this will be made only in those cases where we have reason to suspect serious misspecification in the relationship.

On the basis of this examination of the forecast, both assumptions and adjustments will be reevaluated and another solution produced. The model, with adjustments, will be solved repeatedly, perhaps as many as ten to fifteen times, in trial projections until there are no results that are counterintuitive or until it has been decided by the forecast team that the model is giving a message that cannot be made to agree with intuition. In remarkable circumstances in the past, just preceding the 1969–1970 recession or in first interpreting the oil embargo of 1973, the model appeared to be counterintuitive and resisted all adjustments to make it agree with intuition of no recession on both occasions.[14] After many hard looks at the results, it was decided that the model signaled recession, that intuition was incorrect, and we accepted model conclusions. Those were shining examples of the Wharton model's ability to call a turning point in economic activity well before the realization *but using the adjustment process.*

Steps 9 through 12. Outside Appraisal and Reevaluation

The adjusted model solution is then packaged together with a complete prose statement of all assumptions, covering both input values for exogenous variables and equation adjustments, accompanying tabular quantification of the prose, and a descriptive summary interpretation of the meaning of the results.[15] These constitute the materials that the user panel brings to the forecast seminar, but, of course, they supplement these materials with their own work-a-day results.

Within 2 weeks of receiving the forecast results from the model, the user panel assembles for discussion and critical appraisal. A Wharton meeting opens with prepared statements from people representing a spectrum of economic sectors. These usually cover automobiles, other durable consumer goods, total retail sales, equipment investment, residential construction, steel, petroleum, energy, agriculture, foreign trade, government operations, financial markets, and whatever special sectors are critical areas of the moment. The representatives of these sectors may come from private firms, public agencies, or international bodies. No media personnel are allowed to attend, and frank, plain-spoken language is used to criticize the numerical forecast as deeply, but constructively as possible. Not only do the critics comment on the forecast itself, but they are also often in a position to cite latest results, weekly or monthly, in their own areas of expertise to confirm or refute what the adjusted model results are showing.

Criticism is directed at both assumptions concerning exogenous variables and the forecast paths for endogenous variables. Typically it proves to be impossible to reconcile the views of all participants regarding the outlook for their own industry or sector. All comments and criticisms are recorded by the forecasting group, and on the basis of these criticisms, a new forecast is developed. The postmeeting forecast will involve more indepth analysis of portions of the forecast critiqued in our meeting, as well as updated historical data on the basis of the most recent data releases.

During the meeting, various alternatives to the basic forecast are discussed. These might deal with contingency occurrences from the outside that have lower probability than those assumed for the base case, or they might deal with impending negotiations in halls of legislatures, at bargaining tables, or in diplomatic negotiations.

Step 13 Updating the Forecast

After the forecast meeting—about 1 month after the first data releases on the previous quarter—a new estimate of the last completed quarter is released by official agencies. The results of the forecast meeting are combined with these new data to prepare the postmeeting forecast. One month later, some new data typically become available for the current quarter, and a final forecast exercise is undertaken. There will be three forecasts every quarter, showing the same forecast horizon. The first is a preliminary forecast, the second follows the forecast meeting, and the third is based on the second revision of preliminary data for the most recent quarter. This results in at least one forecast every month— three times per quarter—and an occasional interim forecast to deal with momentous developments in between as needed.

The scheduling of forecast cycles goes something like this:

April, July, October, January 20. Issue of preliminary national income and product accounts for the first, second, third, and fourth quarters, respectively.

May, August, November, February 1. Distribution of preliminary forecast sent to all model users by remote computer access or by mail.

May, August, November, February 15. Holding of forecast seminar.

June, September, December, March 1. Distribution of revised, postmeeting forecast—based on first monthly revision of data.

July, October, January, April 1. Distribution of revised forecast based on latest within-quarter data.

In addition to these monthly releases, there will be special extra releases to deal with unusual or unanticipated events. A good example is President Carter's energy message of April 20, 1977. While new data were being entered for first-quarter performance, an immediate energy program solution was prepared within days following delivery of the message on the basis of data through the fourth quarter of 1976. The fourth-quarter data were used because a few days are normally required to digest properly the preliminary data for a quarter—the first quarter of 1977 in this case—and to update the complete data file for the Wharton model.

In the history of this repetitive approach to economic forecasting by the Wharton group, there have been many unusual events that have required immediate action. Some coincided with a forecast due date; others caused the scrapping of a forecast just completed; while others came at an interim period. They have been

Sterling devaluation, November 1967

Tax surcharge and expenditure control act of 1968

New economic policy, August 1971

Smithsonian Agreement, December 1971

Oil embargo, November 1973

Dropping of controls, May 1974

President Ford's request for tax increase, October 1974

President Ford's budget message, January 1975

Economic stimulus program, January 1977

The Wharton forecast meeting has grown into a highly structured event. At first, the sequence of events was informal and the order of participation was not fixed. But this meeting started with five panel users in 1963 and grew in steps to become a meeting of over 100 people. It is important to stress, though, that all participants have an opportunity to speak to a point of view, commenting, challenging, or supporting views put forward by the Wharton members or the users who speak on their sectors of interest.

The forecast is affected by the meeting. Well-informed users often find flaws in the preliminary forecast, and it is not surprising that 100 critics can bring considerable improvement to an exercise that they monitor carefully in an experienced way. Let us consider some representative forecast-error statistics for early quarter and midquarter Wharton forecasts, the former corresponding to the premeeting and the latter to the postmeeting forecast (see table 4-5).

The left panel provides forecast errors for the amount (level) of real GNP, while the right panel gives the errors for prediction of quarter-to-quarter change (first differences) in real GNP. The fact that the midquarter forecast has some new observed monthly reports that were not available at the time the early quarter forecast was made should contribute toward a reduction in the error for one quarter ahead or possibly two quarters ahead, but should not have as much effect on the forecast beyond that period. The other thing that has changed between these two forecasts is the fact that the forecast meeting has been held. The effect of the meeting on the forecast shows up clearly in the form of persistent improvement.

Not only do the members of the user panel help the econometric forecast, they help each other. The forecast meeting, with its intensive discussion, is a learning process for all participants. Valuable information changes hands and helps all concerned by the exchange.

This is the blend of judgment and quantitative modeling that seems to work well. It is not one person's judgment but that of a whole group that has great continuity of membership from one quarter to the next.

Although the greatest visibility of econometric models in the area of applied analysis is for straight forecasting, there is a closely related application that may be even more important. This related use is in the preparation of alternative simulation projections. As was noted already, there are a number of contingencies that need to be covered, something like the worst and best possible sets of assumptions. Either can occur, but with smaller probability than the central case, or control solution. It is not simply a matter of considering the optimistic and pessimistic alternatives. The computer has made this possible with surprisingly little effort. Once a baseline solution is set up, it is usually fast, cheap, and simple to modify that solution for construction of the alterna-

Table 4-5
Mean Absolute Errors, 1970.3 to 1975.4, Real GNP
(1958 dollars, billions)

Forecast Horizon (Quarters)	Levels						Change					
	1	2	3	4	5	6	1	2	3	4	5	6
Early quarter	4.9	8.6	13.0	16.5	21.3	29.2	4.9	7.4	7.7	8.4	10.0	10.2
Middle quarter	3.9	8.5	13.0	14.7	19.0	25.8	3.9	7.6	7.0	7.9	8.7	10.1

Source: S.K. McNees, *New England Economic Review*, September/October 1976, pp. 30–44.

tives. Some leading input values get changed, but the rest of the solution remains intact and the new case is quickly worked out.

It is conceivable that some new situations may be complicated. Within the framework of a given model, there may not be enough detail to introduce external changes easily or accurately. In the Wharton quarterly model, there is a regulated industry sector, but changed considerations impacting directly on the electric-power sector may be hard to introduce because a partial or fractional change would have to be worked out. It is always possible to go back to the drawing boards and restructure a model by further disaggregation in order to handle the new situation, but that is cumbersome and not fast or cheap. It is therefore recommended that econometric work go in the direction of building large, detailed models that serve general purposes and are available on short notice to accommodate changed considerations that were not foreseen in advance. The largest possible, most detailed system that can be managed and that can produce the main economic magnitudes with preassigned levels of precision is the general-purpose model that is wanted. The issues to be considered in moving in this direction were discussed in chapter 3.

The generating of alternative simulations to compare with the control forecast clarifies the rationale for model adjustment. The factors that make up the adjustment procedures are put into the system to put it on track, to make it realistic, and to improve its forecasting power. But they are to be left in place for the consideration of alternatives. Therefore, the differences among the alternative dynamic-simulation paths compare the effect of the model reactions and not the effect of the adjustment procedures. Since it is usually fast to create alternative simulations, we have a powerful tool that is not generally available to the judgmental economist or pure chartist who lacks a model. Also, many of the alternatives might incorporate a lengthy list of different effects—some on the upside and some on the downside. Unless we have a model that can systematically filter the diverse pieces of information and work out the net effects, we may be at a loss to come to an overall conclusion. Moreover, there is a good reason to believe that errors of forecasting or analysis are smaller for comparison of alternatives than for straight forecasting.

Notes

1. The correction procedure is equivalent to the techniques used in the actual forecasting procedure described later.

2. Clearly these results will not hold exactly unless the model form of the relationship is exactly the estimation form. Frequently, log transformation or scaling are used in the estimated version and the level form in the model. In this case, the residuals from the two sources must be normalized before comparison.

3. See P.J. Dhrymes, *Econometrics: Statistical Foundations and Applications* (New York: Harper and Row, 1970), pp. 227-233.

4. This is discussed later in the chapter and in appendix 4A.

5. The discussion in this section is based on R.M. Young, "Forecasting the U.S. Economy with an Econometric Model," in *Economic Modeling—Current Issues and Problems in Macroeconomic Modeling in the U.K. and U.S.* (London, Heinemann, forthcoming).

6. The term *likely* is used advisedly. Something like the theory of the second best applies to forecasting. As noted, if all single-equation errors are projected correctly, then the system variables will produce the actual path of the economy. It is clear, however, that correct adjustment to all equations, save one, will not necessarily result in a "better" forecast than when correct adjustments are applied to all except n, $n \geqslant 2$.

7. Starting the forecast in period T from an equation in the form of 4.1,

$$\ln y^f_{T+s} = a \sum_{i=0}^{s} b^i + b^{s+1} \ln y_{T-1} + \sum_{i=0}^{s} b^i \, e_{T+s-i}$$

from 4.2

$$\ln y^f_{T+s} = \ln \left[\exp \left(a + b \ln y_{T+s-1}\right) + CON_{T+s}\right]$$

Setting $CON_t = r_t$ and substituting equation 4.4 yields

$$\ln y^f_{T+s} = \ln \left[\exp \left(a + b \ln y_{T+s-1}\right)\right] \exp \left(e_{T+s}\right)$$

$$= a + b \ln y_{T+s-1} + e_{T+s}$$

which is equivalent to the result from equation 4.1.

8. See, for example, S.N. Goldfeld, "The Case of the Missing Money," *Brookings' Papers on Economic Activity,* no. 3, 1976, pp. 683-730; and J. Enzler, L. Johnson, and J. Paulus, "Some Problems of Money Demand," *Brookings' Papers on Economic Activity,* no. 1, 1976, pp. 261-280.

9. The Wharton model uses investment anticipations data directly for forecast periods in which they are available and projects them beyond those periods. See F.G. Adams, and V.J. Duggal, "Anticipations Variables in an Econometric Model, Performance of the Anticipations Version of Wharton Mark III," in L.R. Klein and E. Burmeister (eds.), *Econometric Model Performance* (Philadelphia: Univ. of Pennsylvania, 1976), pp. 9-26.

10. The forecast period projects output starting from initial conditions. Even if percentage changes are correct, the error in the level of output would become even larger and result in increasing errors in the investment sector.

11. The equation depends on the index of prices received by farmers, the unit value index of imported crude materials prices, and the implicit deflator for value added in the mining sector. The specification is constrained by considerations for closing the model.

12. The existence in the model code of an autoregressive disturbance term or lagged dependent variable occasionally causes some confusion. If adjustment of a value from some given path is desired, then it is necessary to calculate carry-over effects in making the adjustment. If, however, we are making an adjustment based on analysis of residuals in an attempt to project disturbances, this is not necessary. For the autoregressive case, the observed residual is

$$e_t = y_t - a - bx_t - \rho(y_{t-1} - a - bx_{t-1})$$

Certainly projection of e_t at a constant value means that accumulation will occur. But if e_t is observed to be approximately constant, we are merely imitating nature, since for the process

$$u_t = \rho u_{t-1} + \bar{e}$$

with $\bar{e}$ constant. We have

$$u_t = \bar{e} \left(\sum_{i=0}^{s} \rho^i \right)$$

Or if we choose to truncate at some value $t = T$,

$$u_{T+s} = \rho^s u_T + \bar{e} \left(\sum_{i=0}^{s} \rho^i \right)$$

which is the form of model accumulation for a constant adjustment. A detailed discussion of the calculations for autoregressive relations appears in appendix 4A.

13. The pattern reflects payment patterns based on expected filing and processing dates.

14. The popular expression for no recession in 1973-1974 was that the economy was coming in for a "soft landing," but the Wharton model group could never find a result that conformed to this view of economic prospects.

15. Appendix 4B contains examples of the "Executive Summary" and a few of the tables mailed to our users. The three mailings sent to quarterly model members during a quarter will contain from 160 to 200 pages of forecast data and from 50 to 75 pages of analytical interpretation.

Appendix 4A
Calculating Adjustments
in the Presence of Lagged
Dependent Variables and
Autoregressive Error
Structures

Let Y_t be a forecast time path defined by

$$Y_t = \beta_0 X_t + \sum_{i=1}^{n} \beta_1 Y_{t-i} + \rho \left(Y_{t-1} - \beta_0 X_{t-1} - \sum_{i=1}^{n} \beta_i Y_{t-1-i} \right)$$

where the third term on the righthand side represents the coding for an autoregressive error term, and where the forecast period runs from 1 to T. Define Y_t^* as an alternate forecast path related to Y_t by

$$Y_t^* = Y_t + \Delta_t \qquad t = 1, \cdots, T$$

To calculate the additive adjustment terms, say, C_t, necessary to achieve Y_t^*, note

$$Y_1^{\,*} = Y_1 + \Delta_1 = Y_1 + C_1$$

$$Y_2^{\,*} = Y_2 + \Delta_2 = \beta_0 X_2 + \beta_1 Y_1^{\,*} + \sum_{i=2}^{n} \beta_i Y_{2-i} + \rho \left[Y_1^* - \beta_0 X_1 \right.$$

$$\left. - \sum_{i=1}^{n} \beta_i Y_{1-i} \right] + C_2$$

Or in general,

$$Y_t^* = Y_t + \Delta_t = \beta_0 X_t + \sum_{i=1}^{t-1} \beta_i Y^*_{t-i} + \sum_{i=t}^{n} \beta_i Y_{t-1}$$

$$+ \rho \left[Y^*_{t-i} - \beta_0 X_{t-1} - \sum_{i=1}^{t-2} \beta_i Y^*_{t-1-i} - \sum_{i=t-i}^{n} \beta_i Y_{t-1-i} \right] + C_t$$

$$= Y_t + \Delta_t = Y_t + \sum_{i=1}^{t-1} \beta_i \Delta_{t-i} + \rho \left[\Delta_{t-1} - \sum_{i=1}^{t-2} \beta_i \Delta_{t-1-i} \right] + C_t$$

Subtracting Y_t from both sides,

$$\Delta_t = \sum_{i=1}^{t-1} \beta_i \Delta_{t-1} + \rho \left[\Delta_{t-1} - \sum_{i=1}^{t-2} \beta_i \Delta_{t-1-i} \right] + C_t$$

or

$$C_t = \Delta_t - \sum_{i=1}^{t-1} \beta_i \Delta_{t-1} - \rho \left[\Delta_{t-1} - \sum_{i=1}^{t-2} \beta_i \Delta_{t-1-i} \right]$$

If an equation is estimated in log-linear form, this calculation becomes a bit more complex.

Let Y_t be a forecast time path generated by

$$Y_t = X_t^{\beta_0} \left(\prod_{i=1}^{n} Y_{t-i}^{\beta_i} \right) (Y_{t-1})^{\rho} \left[X_{t-1}^{\beta_0} \left(\prod_{i=1}^{n} Y_{t-1-i}^{\beta_i} \right) \right]^{-\rho}$$

Again defining Y_t^*, Δ_t, and C_t as earlier, we have

$$Y_1^* = Y_1 + \Delta_1 = Y_1 + C_1$$

$$Y_2^* = Y_2 + \Delta_2 = X_2^{\beta_0} (Y_1 + \Delta_1)^{\beta_1} \left(\prod_{i=2}^{n} Y_{2-i}^{\beta_i} \right) (Y_1 + \Delta_1)^{\rho}$$

$$\left[X_1^{\beta_0} \left(\prod_{t=1}^{n} Y_{1-i} \right) \right]^{-\rho} + C_2$$

Or in general,

$$Y_t^* = Y_t + \Delta_t = X_t^{\beta_0} \left[\prod_{i=1}^{t-1} (Y_{t-i} + \Delta_{t-i})^{\beta_i} \right] \left(\prod_{i=t}^{n} Y_{t-i}^{\beta_i} \right) (Y_{t-1} + \Delta_{t-1})^{\rho}$$

$$\left\{ X_{t-1}^{\beta_0} \left[\prod_{i=1}^{t-2} Y_{t-1-i} + \Delta_{t-1-i} \right)^{\beta_i} \right] \left(\prod_{i=t-1}^{n} Y_{t-1-i} \right)^{\beta_i} \right\}^{-\rho} + C_t$$

Now divide both sides of the preceding equation by Y_t. The first term on the righthand side takes the form

$$X_t^{\beta_0} \left[\prod_{i=1}^{t-1} \left(Y_{t-i} + \Delta_{t-i} \right)^{\beta_i} \right] \left(\prod_{i=t}^{n} Y_{t-i}^{\beta_i} \right) (Y_{t-1} + \Delta_{t-1})^{\rho} \left\{ X_{t-1}^{\beta_0} \left[\prod_{i=1}^{t-2} \right. \right.$$

$$\left. \left. \left(Y_{t-1-i} + \Delta_{t-1-i} \right)^{\beta_i} \right] \left(\prod_{i=t-1}^{n} Y_{t-1-i}^{\beta_i} \right) \right\}^{-\rho}$$

$$\overline{\qquad X_t^{\beta_0} \left(\prod_{i=1}^{n} Y_{t-i}^{\beta_i} \right) (Y_{t-1})^{\rho} \left[X_{t-1}^{\beta_0} \left(\prod_{i=1}^{n} Y_{t-1-i}^{\beta_i} \right) \right]^{-\rho} \qquad}$$

which reduces to

$$\frac{\left[\prod_{i=1}^{t-1} \left(Y_{t-i} + \Delta_{t-i} \right)^{\beta_i} \right] (Y_{t-1} + \Delta_{t-1})^{\rho} \left[\prod_{i=1}^{t-2} \left(Y_{t-1-i} + \Delta_{t-1-i} \right)^{\beta_i} \right]^{-\rho}}{\left(\prod_{i=1}^{t-1} Y_{t-1}^{\beta_i} \right) (Y_{t-1})^{\rho} \left(\prod_{i=1}^{t-2} Y_{t-1-i}^{\beta_i} \right)^{-\rho}}$$

or

$$\left[\prod_{i=1}^{t-1} \left(1 + \frac{\Delta_{t-1}}{Y_{t-i}} \right)^{\beta_i} \right] \left(1 + \frac{\Delta_{t-1}}{Y_{t-1}} \right)^{\rho} \left[\prod_{i=1}^{t-2} 1 + \frac{\Delta_{t-1-i}}{Y_{t-1-i}} \beta_i \right]^{-\rho}$$

Let this equal A_t.

Then

$$1 + \frac{\Delta_t}{A_t} = A_t + \frac{C_t}{Y_t}$$

or

$$C_t = \left(1 + \frac{\Delta_t}{Y_t} - A_t\right) Y_t$$

Notice that the nonlinearity here requires that the values for $Y_1, ..., Y_T$ of the original forecast path be available for the calculation as well as the other data necessary for the linear case.

Appendix 4B
Excerpts from August 31, 1976, Forecast Mailing

The following material was excerpted (without detailed technical notes) from a standard mailing to Wharton members. It illustrates the considerations that went into a forecast just before the presidential election. The Assumptions Memorandum is of particular interest in detailing specification of the assumptions and adjustments that went into this forecast. The memorandum reflects the fact that two control forecasts were produced for this period. The two sample forecast tables reproduced at the end of this Appendix (tables 4B-2 and 4B-3) are those associated with the Wharton interpretation of the Carter economic policy and is described as a "more stimulative policy" (MSP). The other forecast, associated with the Ford administration is referred to as "present policy continued" (PPC) and is not shown.

The Wharton Quarterly Econometric Model, August 31, 1976 Postmeeting Control Forecast Executive Summary

The economy has shifted to a slower rate of expansion than prevailed in late 1975 and early 1976. Following the relatively slow growth rate of 4.27% in constant-dollar GNP in the second quarter, the Wharton model projects a series of quarterly growth rates in the range of 5.0 to 6.5% trending down to the 4.0 to 5.0% range in 1977.

For the remainder of 1976 and 1977 the model shows

1. Growth rates for constant-dollar GNP at 5.0 to 6.0% in 1976 and 4.0 to 5.0% in 1977.
2. Increases in the GNP implicit price deflator of 5.0 to 6.5% during the last half of the current year and 4.5 to 5.0% in 1977. Increases in the consumer price index are expected to be about 6.0% for both 1976 and 1977. The all-commodities wholesale price index should increase less than 5.0% this year and in excess of 6.0% in 1977.
3. An unemployment rate decline to the range of 6.2% by the end of 1977.
4. Continued expansion of corporate profits to $180 billion in 1977.
5. A fall in the federal deficit from $56.0 billion in 1976 to $40.0 billion in 1977.
6. Short-term interest rates gradually increasing about 150 basis points from current levels to mid-1977.
7. The merchandise trade balance remaining negative through all of 1977.

While the outlook for 1977 is relatively independent of the outcome of the election, looking into 1978 and 1979, we see the performance of the economy resting heavily on the economic policies initiated by the next administration to deal with the forecast slowdown in the recovery. Comparing a continuation of current policies with the more stimulative policy package described in the Assumptions Memorandum, we see *current* policy trends leading to

1. Growth in constant-dollar GNP declining to 3.0% in 1978 and to little more than 1.0% in 1979.
2. An unemployment rate falling to approximately 6.0% by the end of 1978 and beginning to rise in early 1979.
3. The rate of increase of the GNP implicit deflator declining to the 5.25% level in early 1979.

A more stimulative policy stance could alter this outlook. The policy assumptions in the current forecast yield

1. Real growth of 4.7% in 1978 declining to 3.0% during the spring quarter of 1979.
2. An unemployment rate that reaches 5.5% by mid-1978 and continues at that level through mid-1979.
3. Inflation rates in the 5.5 to 5.75% range in early 1979.

These findings are summarized in figure 4B-1.

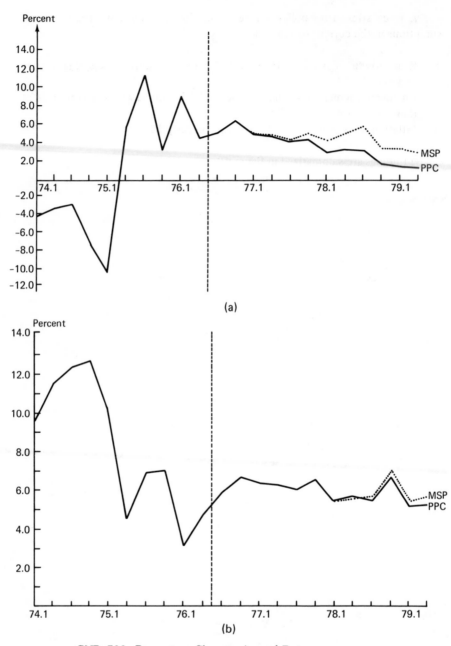

a. GNP, 723—Percentage Change—Annual Rate

b. GNP Implicit Deflator—Percentage Change—Annual Rate

Figure 4B-1. Main Economic Indicators, Historical and Projected.

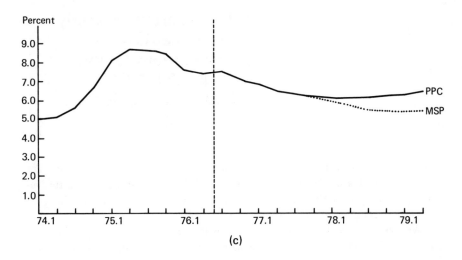

(c)

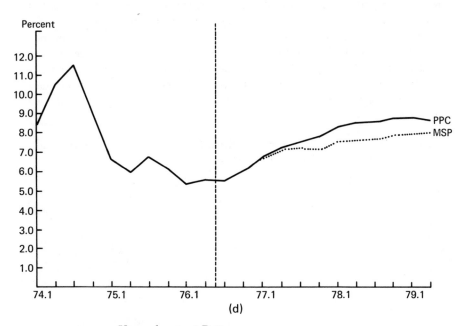

(d)

c. Unemployment Rate
d. 4-6 Month Dealer Placed Commercial Paper Rate

Figure 4B-1. Continued

The Wharton Quarterly Econometric Model, Assumptions for the August 31, 1976 Postmeeting Solutions

This memorandum accompanies two postmeeting forecast solutions. There are two distinctive features to the current release. (1) Each solution covers a twelve-quarter horizon from 1976.3 to 1979.2. (2) Contrary to our normal policy, we have not selected one of the forecasts as a control.

We have followed this course in the belief that the path of the recovery through 1978 and into 1979 has become of more than normal concern to our members. In response to this concern, we extended current policy trends into 1979. As detailed in the Executive Summary and Forecast Review, the Wharton model predicts a substantial slowing in real growth if this policy scenario is pursued. The additional uncertainty attached to the response of a new administration to the perception of this slowdown has led us to produce two control solutions. As detailed below, Control—Present Policies Continued (PPC) assumes that no major policy initiatives occur through mid-1979. The solution Control—More Stimulative Policy (MSP), in addition to more expansive monetary and fiscal policy, includes special initiatives aimed at lowering the unemployment rate and stimulating the housing industry. With the exception of monetary policy, all policy variables assume the same values for FY1977 in the two solutions.

This forecast was prepared by Lawrence R. Klein, F. Garard Adams, Richard M. Young, Dean Chen, Robert S. Chirinko, and Virginia Long.

Principal Assumptions of the WEFA Postmeeting Control Forecast

Federal Budget Assumptions

Federal Government Expenditures

The outlook for the federal budget for FY1977 continues to be uncertain. In addition to the political confrontation between the administration and the Congress, there continues to be some difficulty in interpreting the shortfall of expenditures in FY1976. We assume that some of this shortfall is the result of agencies making decisions as though the transition quarter (TQ) were essentially a fifth quarter in the current fiscal year. Conversations with BEA indicate that the seasonal adjustment for the TQ will in fact be a weighted average of the seasonals for the second and third quarters under the old fiscal year. Some of this TQ bulge will be offset by this downward seasonal adjustment.

As detailed below in table 4B-1, our assumptions for FY1977 are more than $2.0 billion higher than those used in the Premeeting Forecast. While BEA has not published a NIPA translation of the OMB's *Mid-Session Review of the 1977 Budget,* the $400.0 billion projection for outlays on a unified basis appears to translate to a NIPA budget of about $408.0 billion. This is $5.0 billion lower than the $413.3 billion total contained in the *First Concurrent Resolution* and almost $10.0 billion lower than our current projection of approximately $418.0 billion.

Looking toward FY1978, a continuation of current policy trends would lead to NIPA expenditures of $453.7 billion. The package of stimulative policies detailed below increases that expenditure level approximately $8.0 billion to $461.6 billion.

1. Defense Purchases (*GVPFD$*). WEFA projects defense purchases of goods and services of $93.7 billion for FY1977 rising to $102.8 billion in FY1978 under both budget alternatives. The FY1977 total is approximately $1.0 billion higher than either the administration or congressional budgets. These totals include pay increases effective October 1, 1976, 1977, and 1978 of 5, 7.5 and 7.5%, respectively.

2. Nondefense Purchases (*GVPFO$*). We continue to project FY1977 expenditures in this area at just over $48.0 billion. This total is higher than that in the *First Concurrent Resolution* by about $1.0 billion and about $1.5 billion higher than administration proposals. The FY1978 total varies between the two solutions. In the PPC solution this reaches a total of $51.4 billion. In the MSP solution it rises to $59.3 billion. The largest part of the $7.9 billion difference in the two totals is attributable to a more expansive approach to social programs which involves higher employment and expenditure. A small part of the total increase is because of the administrative costs associated with the jobs program described below.

3. Federal Transfers to Persons (*TRGFPRES$*, *TRTOPU$*). Our forecast for transfers is a total of $165.3 billion for FY1977. In FY1978, total transfers actually fall from $178.3 billion in the PPC to $177.6 billion in the MSP as a result of a decline in unemployment transfers, which are endogenous in the model. The forecast total includes assumptions for increases in OASI payments in July of each year. The increases are 6.4% in the current quarter, 5.5% in 1977, and 6.5% in 1978.

4. Federal Government Transfers to Foreigners (*TRGFF$*). At $3.2 billion for both FY1977 and FY1978, these remain below both administration and congressional budget totals. As discussed earlier, both our own and administration forecasts have overstated this recently, and we have consequently lowered our projection.

5. Grants-in-Aid (*GVGIA$*). As noted in the premeeting release, this category accounts for the largest discrepancies between WEFA, administration, and congressional budgets. The *First Concurrent Resolution* budgets $72.9 billion in this category, including substantial funds for public works and jobs programs to be administered at the state level. While the *Mid-Session Review of the 1977 Budget* by OMB has not been translated into NIPA terms by BEA, the total there appears to have risen only slightly from the January budget to about $60.0 billion. We have increased our own projection from the premeeting Forecast by about $1.5 billion to $67.8 billion. Given recent behavior in the unemployment rate, it seems likely that more congressional support will be mustered for legislation and less likely that administrative foot-dragging in expending funds will hold down legislated expenditures. We have made adjustments to our forecast which assume an increase in expenditures and employment by state and local governments. (See Technical Notes and State and Local Government Assumptions for details.) For FY1978, grants-in-aid are assumed to rise to $73.0 billion in both solutions.

6. Net Interest Paid (*YINTGF$*). This is an endogenous variable determined largely by the past history of interest rates and deficits. The forecast for this item varies between solutions in both FY1977 and FY1978. In the former case, the difference is due to the effect of differing monetary policies beginning in 1977.1, as described below. The FY1978 difference can be attributed both to different monetary and fiscal assumptions. The total for FY1977 of about $33.1 billion in both solutions is higher than either the congressional or administration budgets. In FY1978, the total rises to $38.5 billion in the PPC solution and $37.7 in the MSP solution. The lower total in the latter solution is due to a more expansionary monetary policy yielding lower interest rates.

7. Subsidies Less Current Surplus of Government Enterprises (*GVSUBTF$*). The WEFA projection for FY1977 and FY1978, given continuation of current policies (PPC), is for $6.5 billion to be expended in this category. The *Mid-Session Review* indicates a higher total than the administration's January budget, but still is lower than the congressional budget of $6.7 billion. In the MSP solution this item rises to $8.0 billion in FY1978. The additional $1.5 billion is a combination of expenditures on a government-run jobs program and subsidies to the housing industry.

8. Special Assumptions for a More Stimulative Policy (*GVPFO$, NEETTGVF, WBCGVE$, GVSUBTF$, PXGVE, WRCGVFG$*). Federal expenditures are affected in three ways by the policies assumed in the MSP solution. The effects on nondefense purchases and net interest have been described. In addition to the general demand policies of increased federal purchases and easier money, we have assumed that special policies would be initiated to deal with (1) continuing high unemployment rates among certain economic and demographic groups and (2) the generally low level of activity in the housing and construction industry.

First, the jobs program built into the MSP solution assumes that private industry is subsidized to hire people with a long history of unemployment at a wage of $6,000 per annum. It is envisioned that employment would be combined with training. As an inducement to participate in the program, 40.0% of all wages paid to those enrolled in the program in the first year may be credited against corporate taxes. In the second year this credit declines to 20.0%. It is assumed that for each individual enrolled in the program the government incurs $500 in administrative costs with 60.0% being attributable to wages. At the same time that private industry is subsidized to participate, the federal government is assumed to establish separate training programs at a similar wage and administrative cost and run as a government enterprise. This increases government employment and subsidies. We have assumed that this will result in an increase in the deflator for output orginating in government enterprises but not in real output. We have also adjusted the average compensation rates and manhours in such a way that no additional wage or employment increases are generated by the feedbacks from the additional income generated by this policy. We have also adjusted the proportion of income taxed in the lowest bracket to reflect the concentration of the extra income generated by this program.

The division of employment assumed for the two programs is:

	Private	Government	Total
1977.4	25,000	0	25,000
1978.1	75,000	25,000	100,000
1978.2	150,000	75,000	225,000
1978.3	200,000	100,000	300,000
1978.4	250,000	125,000	375,000
1979.1	300,000	150,000	450,000
1979.2	300,000	175,000	475,000

Second, the housing program is aimed at producing an additional 400,000 starts by mid-1979. No specific legislative package is assumed, and higher funding of current programs could well produce this outcome. Based on housing subsidy expenditures in the 1970-1972 period, when subsidized starts averaged nearly 375,000, and a doubling of the price of an average start, we have assumed that increasing housing subsidies $3.0 billion would generate the desired level of starts. In this instance the effective adjustments yield 400,000 additional starts, but higher interest rates reduce nonsubsidized starts such that the total increase from this program is 377,000 starts.

Federal Government Revenues

We continue to assume no major personal tax reduction beyond the extension of the 1975 Revenue Adjustment Act.

1. **Personal Taxes** (*TXCPF*$). It is assumed that provisions of the 1975 Revenue Adjustment Act will be continued through 1979. Collections continue to run ahead of accruals, and adjustments have been made to the tax equation to reflect this and the eventual refunds. Refunds for the earned income credit will continue to be made in the third quarter, and an adjustment has been made to reflect this effect

2. **Corporate Taxes** (*TXCCF*$). We continue to assume no major changes in current corporate profits tax laws. While both the House and Senate versions of the tax bill contain many special provisions, they seem unlikely to have major impacts on the effective corporate tax rates at the level of industrial aggregation contained in the model. Neither these effective tax rates nor the investment tax credit rates are changed during the forecast period. In the MSP solution an adjustment is made to reflect the tax credit associated with the jobs program.

3. **Federal Excise Taxes** (*TXCBF-OIL*$, *TXCBFOIL*$). Provision for the de-

crease in the telephone excise tax in 1977.1 and 1978.1 is included in the forecast. While there has been some discussion concerning the elimination of the small remaining oil import tax, we assume that collections continue at a level of $0.2 billion during the forecast period.

4. Contributions for Social Insurance (*TXCSFT$*). The rate is assumed to remain at current levels until 1978.1. An increase of the combined rate of 0.4% is scheduled to take effect at that point and is allowed for in the forecast. The maximum wage subject to tax is scheduled to rise to $16,500 on January 1, 1977, and our estimate is that the base will rise to $17,700 in 1978.1 based on current legislation. The latter figure will vary with the increase in covered wages for the period 1975.1 and will not be finalized until later this year. An additional increase in the base to $18,900 is assumed in 1979.1.

Monetary Policy

As we have in recent forecasts, in the PPC solution we assume that monetary policy will result in an average increase in the money stock of about 5.5% for 1976 and 8.0% for 1977. The latter figure is well above targeted growth rates announced by the Federal Reserve System, but policies designed to hold growth in the aggregate to levels below this are likely to result in increases in short-term interest rates which are politically and economically unacceptable. Even with this expansion, which runs close to a 9% increase from 1976.2 to 1977.2, we forecast an increase in short-term interest rates of 150 basis points in the next year. In the PPC solution we extend monetary policy to allow for an increase in the last part of 1978 and early 1979 in response to the slowdown in GNP growth rates. This results in a year over year increase in $M1$ of 7.34% from 1977 to 1978. In the MSP solution it is assumed that the new administration can jawbone the Federal Reserve into a more stimulative policy early in 1977 and that the policy pursued would result in short-term rates 100 basis points lower than the PPC solution in the period 1978.3 to 1979.2 *if no other stimulus were applied to the economy*. This policy yields annual growth rates in $M1$ of 5.4%, 9.3%, and 9.2% for 1976, 1977, and 1978, respectively.

State and Local Government

As noted in the August 11, 1976 forecast the July revisions in NIPA revised both the level and rate of growth of purchases of goods and services upward. A further evaluation of trends in this sector has led us to assume that expenditures will increase somewhat faster than previously expected. The $255.2 billion level of purchases assumed for 1977 is a 9.34% increase over the 1976 projection of

$233.4 billion. An additional increase of 8.3% is assumed in 1978. These growth rates in current-dollar expenditures are the same for both solutions and include an allowance for increased expenditures related to the congressional public works program. We assume that the grants are at least partially offset by reductions in expenditures that would have occurred in their absence.

Foreign Trade and the World Economy

Harvest yields in key agricultural producing countries are now perceived with more realism and less guesswork than in spring and midsummer. Last year, the shock of the Soviet harvest failure was a central factor in determining the world outlook for food prices and trade balances. The 1976 harvest looks very encouraging, not only in the United States and the Soviet Union, but also in Asia, for supporting the general world recovery from the 1974–1975 recession. The strengthening of world reserve stocks should stabilize grain prices. Wheat, corn, and rice prices are all on a plateau below their 1973–1974 high values, while soybean prices have risen only moderately from their 1975 low points.

The only danger point has been the drought in Western Europe and Australia. It does not appear that the losses suffered there will strain world reserves, but seasonal fruit, vegetable, and meat prices will show the effects in Europe. Also, world inflation, together with last year's harvest failure, is exerting a significant upward thrust on food prices in communist countries.

France has joined Italy and the United Kingdom as a leading economic trouble spot among industrial countries. This development started in late 1975, but is being exacerbated by this year's drought. France, Italy, and the United Kingdom are all in serious trade deficit and consequently experiencing strong downward pressure on their currency values. Projections for 1976–1977 show a continued deficit position for these three countries, which means that some more devaluation is in store during the next few months. The lire at 1,000 per dollar is a definite possibility by 1977 or 1978. The franc is under the 20-cent mark, while the pound is less than $1.80. There are no real psychological floors until the trade figures improve.

Production, nevertheless, is recovering from recession low points in all three troubled countries. The "real" economies look in all cases better than the "financial" economies. But even the amount of real growth experienced so far has not kept unemployment from rising gradually. The exchange devaluation leads to more domestic inflation and some related austerity programs. If Britain follows through with her announced austerity budget for 1977, and if the Italian government assembles enough political muscle to introduce more spartan measures, we shall be seeing quite modest growth rates for these countries in 1977— only about 2 or 3%. France should likewise slow down a bit in 1977.

The German and Japanese recoveries are proceeding at very healthy rates, sparked by strong export growth and very substantial trade surpluses, in spite of some currency appreciation in mark and yen rates. Present estimates of German and Japanese real growth rates for 1976 are about 6 and 8% respectively, but they should both slow down a bit in 1977.

There is evidence of inflation in socialist countries, rising prices in developing countries, and inflationary effects of exchange devaluation in the deficit-ridden industrial countries. In spite of these evident signs of continuing inflationary pressures, the degree of inflation is coming down a bit throughout the world. Some countries have made dramatic progress in cooling off inflation. Japan is a prime example. Germany and Switzerland remain as bastions of low price profiles, and many countries have come down considerably from the dangerously high points of 1974-1975, although some ground has been lost in recent months. Basic commodity prices are moving, in a mixed pattern, slightly upward, but the extreme speculative pressures of recent years appear to be absent. Also, we can expect another (moderate) turn of the screw by OPEC.

The world prognosis is as follows:

1. A continuation of the recovery in production, but at a slower rate in 1977 than in 1976.
2. A continuation of the tendency toward lower world inflation rates, but with prices moving relentlessly upward.
3. A continuing growth in the volume of world trade.

Agriculture

We continue to expect a moderate rise in farm prices, with the average of the index of prices received by farmers (*PFR**) rising 3.3% this year. Farm prices are expected to be more volatile in 1977 and 1978, with prices rising about 4.25 and 4.5% in these years.

Special Assumptions

1. Petroleum and Natural Gas. The opening of the Alaska pipeline, OPEC price increases, and control and/or decontrol of domestic crude and natural gas prices can all be expected to have a significant impact on the course of output and prices during the current forecast period. These factors also introduce additional uncertainty into the outlook as a result of the difficulty of evaluating their timing and magnitude.

We continue to assume a 10% OPEC price increase effective January 1, 1977, with further price increases of 7.5% January 1, 1978 and January 1, 1979.

In connection with the first price hike, we have assumed some forward shifting of imports.

The Energy Policy and Conservation Act, which required a rollback in the price of domestic oil to an average price of $7.66 per barrel, provided that FEA monitor the price controls through receipts. Data for the period February through June indicate that due to a change in the mix of upper- and lower-tier oil and transactions prices for upper-tier oil in excess of the ceiling, the average price of oil exceeded the allowed ceiling. As a consequence, FEA has frozen the ceiling price at June levels until cumulative receipts match those which would have been received if average price had followed the desired path, that is, $7.66 plus increases equal to the rate of inflation of the GNP implicit deflator plus a 3% production incentive. Recent legislation extending the life of FEA imposes a 10% limit on the annual rate of increase in the ceiling prices. An additional complication in petroleum pricing arises from the decontrol of tertiary oil and oil from stripper wells, which account for some 10 to 15% of domestic production.

It is expected that the pipeline will be tested and filled on schedule and that shipment will start in 1977.3. In this forecast we assume that flows are initially at a level of 400,000 barrels per day rising by stages to 1,500,000 barrels per day in 1978.2. We also assume that the entire output of the pipeline displaces imports rather than domestic production elsewhere. There is some uncertainty about the price at which the Alaskan oil will be sold. We have assumed that it will enter the market at the average control price rather than the upper-tier price.

The recent FPC ruling changing the price regulations on interstate natural gas sales has proven very difficult to evaluate. Reliable statistics on the interstate flows by vintage do not appear to be readily available. Moreover, estimates of how the increase in price is likely to affect new sources and the mix between inter-state and intrastate sales exhibit extraordinarily large variances. In lieu of any firm data on which to make a judgment, we have assumed that the ruling will increase the rate of increase in the deflator for output originating in the mining sector by approximately 0.5%.

2. Holder-in-Due-Course. As in the last two forecasts, we assume the affects of the FTC ruling will be to temporarily depress purchases in certain durables categories while dealers in the retail and financial markets adjust to the new regulations. A detailed summary of our reasoning on these effects appeared in the June 1 Assumptions Memorandum, which can be referred to for details.

3. Residential Structures. We continue to adjust for the impact of various federal government programs in our housing-starts equations. Under the impact of rising interest rates and the expiration of these programs, starts drop precipitously in late 1977 and early 1978. It appears reasonable to expect some new initiatives in this area at that time, but until some indication of the form these might take becomes apparent, it is difficult to adjust for such a program. We have assumed for the PPC forecast that no additional subsidies to housing are budgeted beyond current programs.

As discussed earlier, the MSP solution assumes that some new initiatives will be made in the housing area in FY1978 resulting in an additional 400,000 starts by mid-1979.

Table 4B-1
WEFA Federal Budget Assumptions,
August 31, 1976, Postmeeting Control Forecast

	WEFA Budget—Present Policies Continued			WEFA Budget—More Stimulative Policy	
	Transition Quarter 1976.3 Annual Rate	Fiscal 1977	Fiscal 1978	Fiscal 1977	Fiscal 1978
Purchases	135.3	141.9	154.3	141.9	162.1
Defense	88.7	93.7	102.8	93.7	102.8
Nondefense	46.6	48.3	51.4	48.3	59.3
Transfers	164.1	168.5	181.5	168.5	180.8
To persons	160.9	165.3	178.3	165.3	177.6
To foreigners (net)	3.2	3.2	3.2	3.2	3.2
Grants in aid	61.9	67.8	73.0	67.8	73.0
Net interest	28.5	33.2	38.5	33.1	37.7
Subsidies less current surplus of government enterprises	6.0	6.5	6.5	6.5	8.0
Wage disbursements less accruals	0.0	0.0	0.0	0.0	0.0
Total expenditures (NIPA basis)	395.8	417.9	453.7	417.8	461.6
Adjustments to unified	−5.0	−11.0	−11.0	−11.0	−11.0
Total expenditures (unified basis)	390.8	406.9	442.7	406.8	450.6
Total revenues (NIPA basis)	339.8	373.2	424.0	373.3	428.1
Adjustments to unified	−12.0	−13.0	−13.0	−13.0	−13.0
Total revenues (unified basis)	327.8	360.2	411.0	360.3	415.1
Surplus or deficit (−) (NIPA basis)	−56.0	−44.7	−29.7	−44.5	−33.5
Surplus or deficit (−) (unified basis)	−63.0	−46.7	−31.7	−46.5	−35.5

Table 4B–2

Sample Table from EFA Forecast: Selected Major Economic Indicators

Line Var Label		Item	1976.2	1976.3	1976.4	1977.1	1977.2
1 GNP$	I	Gross National Product	1674.1	1719.7	1774.8	1825.1	1874.8
2 GNP$	I	% Chg Gross National Product	9.59	11.15	13.45	11.84	11.33
3							
4 GNP	I	Real Gross National Product	1259.4	1275.4	1295.4	1311.6	1326.9
5 GNP	I	% Chg Real Gross National Product	4.27	5.18	6.41	5.10	4.75
6							
7 YN$	I	National income	1336.3	1376.2	1423.4	1464.6	1505.0
8							
9 YP$	I	Personal income	1362.0	1399.0	1439.3	1477.5	1517.8
10							
11 PDGNP	I	Implicit price deflator = GNP	132.9	134.8	137.0	139.2	141.3
12 PDGNP	I	% Chg Implicit GNP Deflator	5.09	5.86	6.61	6.41	6.28
13							
14 PXP	I	Implicit price deflator = private GNP	133.1	135.0	137.2	139.4	141.6
15 PXP	I	% Chg Private GNP Deflator	5.02	6.08	6.17	6.65	6.50
16							
17 PC*	B	% Chg Consumer price index	5.04	5.88	6.09	6.59	5.95
18 PW*	B	% Chg Wholesale price index	6.08	6.04	4.63	7.29	5.54
19							
20 RAXNMPV	I	Private output per manhour	8.68	8.75	8.82	8.86	8.90
21 RAXNMPV	I	% Chg Private output per manhour	4.09	3.23	3.41	1.82	1.83
22							
23 WRCPV$	I	Private compensation per manhour	6.54	6.67	6.81	6.97	7.11
24 WRCPV$	I	% Chg private compensation/manhour	8.83	7.80	8.89	9.42	8.57
25							
26 NRUT	B	Unemployment rate (%)	7.43	7.49	7.17	6.83	6.55
27							
28 TBB$	I	Net exports, current $	8.1	5.1	0.4	–5.0	–4.1
29							
30 FM1$	I	Money supply = M1	302.7	306.6	314.5	321.6	328.9
31 FM1$	I	% Chg money supply = M1	8.63	5.23	10.70	9.34	9.37
32 FM2$	I	Money supply = M2	696.5	713.0	732.5	749.9	766.7
33 FM2$	I	% Chg money supply = M2	11.83	9.81	11.37	9.86	9.27
34							
35 FRMTB3MY	B	3 Month treasury bill rate	5.16	5.17	5.77	6.36	6.67
36 FRMCUAAAN	B	Corp AAA Utility bond rate	8.67	8.46	8.46	8.39	8.28
37 FRMPRIME	B	Prime rate for large businesses	6.90	6.72	7.01	7.53	8.08
38 FRMCP4M	B	4–6 Mon commercial paper rate	5.57	5.48	6.00	6.62	7.08
39 FRMCS	B	Moody's total corp bond rate	9.05	8.90	8.82	8.74	8.65
40							
41 YPDSAVR	I	Personal savings rate (%)	7.10	6.79	6.59	6.46	6.40
42							
43 CPUBT$	I	Corporate profits before tax	145.3	156.1	167.3	174.6	178.7
44							
45 GVSURPF$	I	Federal surplus, NIA basis	–53.5	–56.1	–51.3	–45.9	–41.9

[a]Wharton Mark 4.2 Quarterly Model Postmeeting Control–More Stimulative Policy–August 31, 1976.

1977.3	1977.4	1978.1	1978.2	1978.3	1978.4	1979.1	1979.2	1976	1977	1978
1922.1	1976.3	2023.3	2076.9	2135.5	2190.9	2238.9	2287.1	1701.2	1899.6	2106.7
10.48	11.77	9.86	11.02	11.78	10.79	9.05	8.89	12.19	11.66	10.90
1340.7	356.7	1370.8	1388.1	1407.7	1419.8	1431.9	1442.3	1269.1	1334.0	1396.6
4.22	4.88	4.21	5.14	5.79	3.48	3.43	2.95	6.50	5.11	4.70
1542.8	1587.7	1625.5	1669.8	1718.7	1764.1	1801.9	1839.1	1360.1	1525.0	1694.5
1561.5	1605.7	1638.3	1680.7	1731.8	1778.5	1814.3	1852.4	1382.9	1540.6	1707.3
143.4	145.7	147.6	149.6	151.7	154.3	156.4	158.6	134.0	142.4	150.8
6.00	6.57	5.42	5.59	5.66	7.07	5.43	5.77	5.36	6.23	5.93
143.7	145.9	148.0	150.1	152.3	154.6	156.7	159.1	134.2	142.7	151.2
6.19	6.30	5.65	5.94	5.96	6.09	5.70	6.09	5.09	6.32	6.01
5.89	5.87	5.55	5.51	5.71	5.64	5.59	5.70	5.75	6.06	5.69
7.27	7.02	7.42	6.39	7.50	6.92	8.01	6.16	4.81	6.21	6.99
8.94	8.98	9.01	9.05	9.11	9.14	9.17	9.21	8.71	8.92	9.08
1.40	1.98	1.34	1.90	2.60	1.22	1.33	1.74	3.93	2.41	1.78
7.25	7.39	7.55	7.69	7.84	7.99	8.15	8.31	6.61	7.18	7.77
7.93	8.03	8.70	7.62	8.27	7.76	8.09	8.23	7.86	8.65	8.15
6.34	6.12	5.95	5.75	5.53	5.50	5.47	5.49	7.43	6.46	5.68
−5.3	−4.5	−3.3	−0.5	2.3	3.7	2.2	1.6	5.5	−4.7	0.6
338.2	344.9	351.8	360.1	368.4	376.2	384.7	394.7	305.1	333.4	364.1
11.76	8.16	8.36	9.72	9.50	8.84	9.26	10.82	5.40	9.27	9.23
785.6	802.3	818.7	836.4	854.3	871.6	889.6	909.4	704.8	776.1	845.3
10.23	8.78	8.44	8.93	8.83	8.36	8.50	9.20	9.97	10.12	8.91
6.68	6.55	7.04	7.02	7.04	7.27	7.39	7.34	5.25	6.56	7.09
8.21	8.00	7.93	7.93	7.95	7.93	7.93	7.96	8.56	8.22	7.94
8.30	8.32	8.52	8.67	8.76	8.91	9.02	9.07	6.87	8.06	8.72
7.14	7.09	7.45	7.54	7.57	7.78	7.85	7.86	5.59	6.98	7.59
8.56	8.42	8.31	8.25	8.22	8.19	8.17	8.17	9.00	8.59	8.24
6.38	6.36	5.97	5.92	6.10	6.15	5.89	5.64	6.85	6.40	6.04
182.8	188.0	188.7	193.8	201.6	203.5	205.1	207.0	152.4	181.0	196.9
−39.1	−38.4	−32.1	−31.0	−32.4	−29.9	−23.7	−17.6	−56.2	−41.3	−31.4

Table 4B–3

Sample Table from EFA Forecast: Gross National Product in Constant Dollars

Line Var Label		Item	1976.2	1976.3	1976.4	1977.1	1977.2
1 GNP	I	Gross National Product	1259.4	1275.4	1295.4	1311.6	1326.9
2							
3 CE	I	Personal consumption expend	808.6	817.5	828.2	837.3	846.2
4 CED	I	Durable goods	125.2	126.7	129.5	131.1	132.6
5 CEN	I	Nondurable goods	317.6	320.6	324.0	327.1	330.1
6 CES	I	Services	365.8	370.3	374.7	379.1	383.4
7							
8 IBT	I	Gross private domestic invest	171.7	177.8	188.8	197.5	203.2
9 IBF	I	Fixed investment	160.6	165.8	174.5	182.9	188.9
10 IBFN	I	Nonresidential	114.9	118.0	123.9	129.8	135.5
11 IBFR	B	Residential structures	45.7	47.8	50.6	53.1	53.5
12							
13 IBIT	I	Chg in business inventories	11.1	12.0	14.4	14.6	14.2
14							
15 TBB	I	Net exports	15.4	12.8	9.7	6.4	6.3
16 TEB	I	Exports	94.7	94.4	94.4	94.8	96.5
17 TMB	I	Imports	79.3	81.6	84.7	88.4	90.2
18							
19 GVPT	I	Govt purchases of goods and services	263.6	267.2	268.7	270.3	271.3
20 GVPF	I	Federal	96.0	98.2	98.6	98.9	98.8
21 GVPFD	I	National defense	63.6	64.3	64.9	65.2	65.3
22 GVPFD	I	Other	32.3	33.8	33.7	33.8	33.5
23 GVP$	I	State and local	167.7	169.0	170.1	171.4	172.5

[a]Wharton Mark 4.2 Quarterly Model Postmeeting Control—More Stimulative Policy—August 31, 1976.

1977.3	1977.4	1978.1	1978.2	1978.3	1978.4	1979.1	1979.2	1976	1977	1978
1340.7	1356.7	1370.8	1388.1	1407.7	1419.8	1431.9	1442.3	1269.1	1334.0	1396.6
855.4	865.1	874.0	883.3	892.8	901.6	909.6	916.7	813.7	851.0	887.9
134.7	137.3	140.0	142.7	145.1	147.4	149.4	150.9	126.4	133.9	143.8
333.1	335.9	338.5	341.2	344.1	346.8	349.2	351.2	319.2	331.6	342.7
387.6	391.8	395.6	399.5	403.5	407.5	411.0	414.5	368.1	385.5	401.5
207.7	211.0	212.0	214.1	217.0	220.4	223.6	226.6	176.4	204.8	215.9
193.2	195.6	197.2	199.6	202.8	206.2	209.6	212.9	164.4	190.2	201.4
140.8	145.3	148.8	152.1	155.4	158.7	161.9	164.7	117.3	137.9	153.7
52.4	50.3	48.4	47.5	47.4	47.5	47.7	48.2	47.1	52.3	47.7
14.5	15.4	14.8	14.5	14.2	14.2	14.0	13.8	12.0	14.7	14.4
5.1	4.8	5.2	5.9	7.3	7.0	5.9	4.7	13.6	5.7	6.4
98.2	100.5	103.1	106.2	108.7	110.7	112.5	113.5	94.3	97.5	107.2
93.1	95.7	97.9	100.2	101.4	103.7	106.7	108.8	80.7	91.9	100.8
272.5	275.9	279.7	284.7	290.7	290.8	292.7	294.3	265.3	272.5	286.5
98.9	101.4	104.2	108.4	113.3	112.6	113.5	114.3	97.0	99.5	109.6
65.5	66.5	67.2	68.4	69.1	68.3	69.0	69.7	64.1	65.6	68.2
33.4	34.9	37.1	40.0	44.2	44.3	44.4	44.6	32.9	33.9	41.4
173.6	174.5	175.4	176.3	177.3	178.2	179.2	180.0	168.3	173.0	176.8

5 How Well Have We Done?

However good is the qualitative judgment of myself or some person who follows events more closely than I, our judgment has been formed and is kept tuned up by looking at computer forecasts. I would no more dream of tackling the back of an envelope before I had looked at the Wharton, and Michigan, and St. Louis Models than I would dream of doing so on the basis of tea-leaves or rereading Alfred Marshall's Principles. *In other words, we dwarfs of judgment see as far as we do because we stand on the shoulders of computer giants.*[1]

The builders of the earliest national econometric models in the late 1930s and 1940s would have regarded today's developments and model uses as utterly unbelievable. Those who have taken part in this evolution had to be believers and project a possible development that could come only with new data bases, improved theorizing (economic and statistical inference), and better facilities, but even they never expected to achieve the degree of precision or enjoy the acceptability that has been accorded to this art/science today. There is no doubt that the high-speed electronic computer, with massive memory, played an instrumental role, together with data preparation, macroeconomic analysis, and econometric theory, in making the situation of today possible.

Apart from a few scattered scholars in research institutes and sparse offerings of econometrics teaching at some leading universities, at that time there was no semblance of an "industry" as we know it today. Now there are many textbooks, abundant teaching offerings at all levels of study (graduate and undergraduate), and many models in active use. There are many ways to judge the degree of success of this subject, but one way of looking at the matter is to go by the "test of the market" for the "econometrics industry." Other more professional tests will also be taken up in this chapter, but let us first look at the market.

In the United States alone, there is a multimillion dollar market of econometric simulations—forecasts, policy analyses, data banks, computer software packages, and private consultations. A rough estimate of this commercial sector puts gross sales for 1977 at $30 million to $40 million, and it is growing fast. This does not include all the special-purpose econometric studies being done by private investigators (academic and other) or inhouse econometric studies by government and business. The Wharton model forecasts were made available to private corporations in 1963 and have met the test of the market ever since that time, with competitors joining to share a rapidly expanding market in the 1970s.

131

The relevance of the market test is simply this: cold, calculating enterprises who are very cost (and revenue) conscious would not have kept subscribing to these services, year in and year out for almost 15 years if they were not getting something useful from them—something that adds a dimension not readily achievable by other approaches. It would certainly not be achievable by purely qualitative or judgmental economic analysis. Significant business-cycle downturns in 1969 and 1973, both forecasted well in advance by the Wharton model, followed by large-scale costcutting by business, never cut seriously into the growth of the econometrics industry.

Not only in the private sector has there been an enormous increase in the use of econometric models in business analysis, but also in the public sector there has been a rapidly growing use in policy formation. This public-sector growth has taken place at the federal level, at the state/local government level, and internationally, among the large organizations as well as foreign governments. What has been true of the United States is now taking place in Europe, Australia, Canada, Mexico, Japan, and practically everywhere in the world.

Private Use of Econometric Models

In a preceding chapter we indicated how the Wharton model goes through the stages of a forecasting exercise. Now we look at the applications from the other end, the private-user end. First and foremost, private corporations who are in a national market must forecast national economic tendencies, including both short-term fluctuations and longer-term trends. A national corporation must have foresight and insight into purely national magnitudes as well as its own industry or sector variables. Almost everyone is interested in GNP, the inflation rate, interest rates, the unemployment rate, and other main aggregates, but as they get involved in more analytical work about the economy, staff members with large-scale enterprises have to stay in touch with scores or even hundreds of related magnitudes—wage rates, production by sector, raw material flows, productivity, capital formation by type, and so on. The company economist or staff equivalent must be prepared to report at any time on the detailed state of the economy to the boards of top management.

For an analysis and forecast of their own or a related sector model, the private company economist must estimate linking relations to show how his own company or industry model is driven by the national model. As an example,

$$S_i = f_i(S, S_j, p_i/p)$$

where S_i = ith sector's sales

S = national sales (corresponding line of activity)

p_i = ith sector's price

p = national price index

This relation states that sales by the ith sector depend on national sales, related sector j's sales, and the price relative of sector i. Other specific variables that are closely tied to sector i's activity may also be considered for inclusion in f_i. This form of analysis could apply to company i or region i. It is stated, as an example, for sales but is applicable to output, employment, price, wage, or other variables. Complete interrelated models of the sector or region may be constructed too, but simple linking relations like the preceding are an easy first approximation. In the case of individual companies, they are often expressed as market-share relations. The main point for present purposes, however, is clear. A national model generates values of variables such as S and p that can be used as input values in forecasting relevant magnitudes for sector i or firm i, and this is a frequent activity in applied econometrics for a private-sector user of a national econometric model.

A local-area model user may not be in the national market directly but is strongly affected by national economic events. In such cases, it is important to have access to a national model in order to develop the broader input values to drive local relationships or a whole local model. Wharton models of metropolitan areas (Philadelphia and New York) and states (Georgia, Kentucky, Mississippi) are used in this mode.

Forecasting applications are obvious and, in a sense, straightforward. Simulation exercises for "what if" alternatives, policy options, or scenarios are equally important uses, probably more important than straight forecasting. Although it may not be apparent, large, national corporations in the private sector are also major users of such alternative simulations. The large corporation has an immediate stake in national tax alternatives, personal or business. To some extent it is a matter of their social interest and to some extent it is a matter of their (indirect) self-interest. Economic analysts for large corporations rightfully busy themselves with a complete range of national policy issues. A national econometric model is a natural tool for analysis of the issues.

Even if a private-sector user is not among the largest corporations with a full-size economic staff, it may take up national policy problems directly or study them through the medium of a trade association or similar business confederation. Large, private-sector users, therefore, are business associations who use the pooled resources of smaller members. National model policy simulations are of direct interest to them, as are sector models.

Public Use of Econometric Models

Management or monitoring of the whole national economy is the job of many federal agencies. They are directly interested in forecasts and policy simulations at the national level. It is important that they have the ability to respond quickly to requests for information on the economic effects of new legislation, administration proposals, contingent possibilities, or major disturbances. The publicly maintained models are used for these purposes, but the privately supplied models are regularly subscribed to on a broad basis within government. Policy simulation of internal and external models is part of the everyday work schedule in several Washington offices

Just as the private firm has its special area or preserve in a given sector served by that firm or in a model of the company itself, so do federal agencies have well-defined, limited areas of interest. An agricultural model is used by the Department of Agriculture, an energy model by the Department of Energy, commodity models by the stockpile manager (General Services Administration), a labor market model by the military, and a model of the Soviet Union by the intelligence community. Wharton econometric models have been constructed in all these cases. The specialized models take inputs from the economy as a whole, generated by the national Wharton model, and use them to power the restricted-area model. In the case of the energy system, that is done in a full simultaneous system with feedback between the national economy and the energy sector. Senior government officers are briefed on the economic outlook and policy simulations by economists who have been using econometric models in much the same way that company officers are briefed with similar materials in the private sector. Federal economic policy is not made directly on the basis of model results, but model results are used together with less formal analysis, and all the information is put together before a decision is reached. It is, nevertheless, a fact that model results are among the most important in reaching policy decisions.

State and local users of models have a variety of interests, but there is one predominant application that holds their attention, namely, to forecast revenues of their own political subdivisions. To a large extent, practitioners in state or local area revenue offices can make reasonably good projections of revenues if they can pin down the revenue base. This may be an income level, sales turnover, real property valuation, or other asset valuation. Many of these base calculations may be extracted directly from a national model, but the relevance of such macro projections depends on the size and representativeness of the region. A two-step procedure is preferable. The national model drives a local-area model, and the local-area model generates local-area revenue bases. If a full, local-area model is being used, then the revenue equations should be built right into the model specification. It is an oversimplification to say that state and local revenue offices can project revenues quite well if they start from a good estimate of the appropriate revenue base. Further refinements can be developed to good advantage because revenue provisions are getting more varied outside the national scene.

From the home state of the Wharton model a good set of "linking" equations can be designed to show how major components of state revenues can be directly related to aggregate magnitudes that are generated from the national quarterly model, thus permitting fiscal-year phasing into a national quarterly forecast (see, for example table 5-1).

Table 5-1
Pennsylvania Personal Income Tax Linking Equation

$$\ln PAPIT = -0.256 + 0.173Q_1 + 0.338Q_2 + 0.054Q_3 + 0.152D + 0.815\ln(YP - TRTOP\$)$$
$$(0.26) \quad (6.88) \qquad (13.31) \qquad (2.15) \qquad (4.65) \qquad (5.75)$$

$\bar{R}^2 = 0.917$
$SEE = 0.0373$
$DW = 1.89$

$PAPIT$	= Pennsylvania personal income tax collection
Q_i	= quarterly (seasonal indicator; $Q_i = 1$ in quarter i, otherwise zero
D^i	= indicator for lowering of tax rates in 1974.1; $D = 1$ on or before 1974.1, otherwise zero
$YP - TRTOP\$$	= U.S. personal income less transfer payments

Apart from adjustments for the seasonal quarter or changes in tax laws, the equation in table 5-1 says that Pennsylvania taxes follow national personal (nontransfer) income. This variable is regularly generated in forecast mode by solutions of the Wharton model. The "elasticity" is 0.815. A 10% change in personal income generates an 8% change in Pennsylvania's tax collection, on average.

Although this is not the actual equation used by the state revenue authorities, it could be used by them and has, in fact, been used for purposes of checking some revenue forecasts. Similar equations have been estimated for Pennsylvania sales taxes and corporate net income taxes.

While the focus of attention is on the projections of revenues, the flow of expenditures can vary to a certain extent with the level of area activity. Transfer payments for welfare, income security, retirement, and medical services vary regularly with economic activity. They too have to be projected, just as revenues must be projected; so this puts additional demands on model use.

In the case of national policy planning, decisionmakers have to allow for the feedback effects of their actions on economic performance of the economy as a whole. This is less of a problem at the state level and probably not a major issue at the most refined local level. The economic environment may be taken largely as given, and then adaptations of state or local government reactions to them are studied through the model. Major economic policy affecting the overall performance of the economy is not taken at much less than the national level unless large groupings of states act together. But models are used in the process of state economic planning—to meet the needs as required of the educational system, the system of public services, and the welfare department. They may also be used to analyze the potential for attracting industry or general population movements.

The localized models of a state, city, or other political subdivision are used mostly by public authorities, but they simultaneously serve the needs of private-sector users who operate in a restricted area. Typical users in this category are newspapers, banks, department stores, port authorities, utility systems, chambers of commerce, welfare funds, and local foundations. They generally want to help communities in which they operate and use local models in the furthering of this kind of aim, but they also use them in planning in their own enterprises.

The Track Record

Econometric models have been used and will be used in increasing amounts in both the private and public sectors. In this sense they have established their worth, but what do the quantitative measures of success show in model terms, not in sales revenue terms? In a broad sense, models are used as prediction or forecasting tools, but only the forecasts of actual events can be compared with outcome values to determine some kind of success ratios. As has been emphasized here, among the greatest uses are the simulation of alternatives. These do not lend themselves easily to checking against reality, since only one of the alternatives actually can be observed. Moreover, if policy analysis through model simulation is used to devise schemes that are preventive against adversity, econometric success cannot actually or strictly be validated because the undesired positions for the economy ought not to occur. We can never be sure about what would have happened if model advice were not heeded, when it actually is, or vice versa. On the other hand, it may be possible to collect adverse evidence if model simulations predict undesired outcomes in the absence of policy moves and if the policy advice is ignored while the undesired consequences do not develop.

The problem of evaluating the forecasting accuracy of econometric models has many facets, including the notion that models are now having an impact on policy decisions that will substantially affect the outlook. The question most often asked is how accurate are the forecasts made using the model, disregarding questions of policy assumptions and other exogenous inputs. Naive conclusions are often reached regarding the quality of a model on the basis of its forecasting record. With the practices described earlier, forecast accuracy clearly involves not just the issue of how well the model represents economic behavior, but also evaluation of how well the model user uses that particular model. An excellent model may be used to produce bad forecasts for a variety of reasons, including assumptions about exogenous variables and adjustment inputs. Alternatively, a bad model may be used by a forecaster with insight and intuition to produce an accurate forecast if the user freely modifies adjustments to force the model to conform to his or her intuition.

A further problem involves the identification of the model. We refer to "the" Wharton quarterly model, but the model and its structure are continuously evolving through time. The model contained just over 300 variables as recently as 1971, compared with 1,000 in the present version. This growth has not been the result of a simple disaggregation, but rather an elaboration and re-structuring of causal relationships. The influence of financial variables, relative prices, and demographics follow much different paths and have different quantitative effects in the present version of the model compared with earlier versions. These changes are evolutionary rather than revolutionary, but they do imply that forecasts made at points in time, 4 to 5 years apart, are being made with model structures that differ in substantive matters. They can be called *generational* differences.

It is also true that the personnel in the forecasting group changes. In any econometric forecasting group with a strong methodological framework, personalities are likely to affect the forecast less than in a purely judgmental environment. It is impossible to eliminate personal bias from the techniques described in chapter 4, but adherence to the evaluation methods described seems likely to minimize this effect on the forecast.

If the same forecasting group using the same forecasting methodology at the same time and with the same information set could forecast with a variety of models, forecasting accuracy could be used as a test for model validation. In the absence of such a test, firm conclusions regarding the "goodness" of a model or group of models cannot be reached on the basis of reported forecast errors. Only actual model users are likely to be able to evaluate the model structure based on their own forecasting experience.

Nevertheless, in spite of the generational changes, the rotating of personnel, and the evolution of the Wharton models, performance appears to be fairly steady over a period of 16 years, by quarters. If some members of the model team are temporarily absent, the work continues with the established methodology and produces practically the same kinds of forecasts.

It is worth pointing out that many economist-statisticians like to study ex post forecast error for the purpose of model validation. That is an exercise of computing what the model forecast *would have been* if subsequent inputs for initial conditions and exogenous variables had been the latest revised estimates, that is, as accurate as possible. We then ask *what would have been* the forecast if we know what we now know but did not at forecast time? This is an interesting question but is hypothetical and lacks reality. We never know what we actually would have done if circumstances had been different. The payoff in model use is not in rehashing history but in being as right as possible about unknown futures. It is not a one-time or seldom event; it is replication. In the case of the Wharton model, it is a record that has been built from quarterly forecasts ever since 1963—more than 60 replications with many different variables.

The forecast error is the difference between the actual value assumed by an item of interest in any given period and the predicted value. This seemingly straightforward assertion leaves unanswered many questions about the appropriate techniques for measuring or summarizing the error.[2]

First is the issue of what is the actual value that should be used in calculating the error. National Income and Product Account (NIPA) data, including the wide range of official statistics, are in a continual state of revision. Should one use the latest estimates? Or the first estimates? The latter have been suggested as appropriate on the grounds that they have the largest influence on current economic decisions Using the latest data means that the source data for error calculations will have been through differing numbers of revisions, and computed errors will change when later estimates become available. However, it seems likely that forecast users are more interested in what actually has happened than in what the first guess about what has happened will be. For either descriptive or comparative purposes, the latest observations on actual data seem more relevant.

A further problem raised by data revisions concerns what it is that is being forecast. Even if we agree that the error should be calculated on the basis of the most recent data, we must still decide whether the forecast concerns the level or change in the economic variable of interest. To illustrate the problem, suppose that at the time of the forecast, say, time t, the latest actual observation is A_{t-1}^*, and given this initial value, the forecast values are

$$A_t^f, A_{t+1}^f, \ldots, A_{t+n}^f$$

At the time $t + n + 1$ we have historical data

$$A_{t-1}, A_t, A_{t+1}, \ldots, A_{t+n}$$

where $A_{t-1}^* \neq A_{t-1}$

that is, the data for period $t - 1$ have been revised. If we are interested in evaluating the error in the predicted change, it seems likely that the appropriate comparison is predicted change to actual change, that is:

$$A_t^f - A_{t-1}^* \quad \text{to} \quad A_t - A_{t-1}$$
$$A_{t+1}^f - A_t^f \quad \text{to} \quad A_{t+1} - A_t$$
$$A_{t+n}^f - A_{t+n-1}^f \quad \text{to} \quad A_{t+n} - A_{t+n-1}$$

No adjustment is made to the data except for the predicted change in the first period, which is based on the known starting point at the time of the forecast rather than the latest (revised) estimate. For level calculations we might want to make an equivalent adjustment. When comparing A_t^f to A_t, we might ask what the forecast level would have been if the forecast change had been the same but we had had A_{t-1} as the estimate of the lag rather than A_{t-1}^*. This may result in an error measure based on a comparison of

$$A^f_t + (A_{t-1} - A^*_{t-1}) \quad \text{to} \quad A_t$$
$$A^f_{t+1} + (A_{t-1} - A^*_{t-1}) \quad \text{to} \quad A_{t+1}$$
$$A^f_{t+n} + (A_{t-1} - A^*_{t-1}) \quad \text{to} \quad A_{t+n}$$

This is clearly an arbitrary adjustment, but the general problem admits of no unique solution.

There is also a dimension to the changes versus levels measurement of error beyond the issue of data revisions. This arises because there is no unique relationship between multiperiod level and the associated change forecasts. To illustrate the problem, two forecasters may project the two-quarter change in GNP to be 100, but have very different changes in the two quarters, say, 50 and 50 versus 25 and 75. These two forecasts would have the same two-period-level error but different errors for the quarter-by-quarter changes. Level predictions can also be incorrect by a *biased* amount, yet change predictions can be quite correct.

Further issues in error analysis involve both the units of measurement and summary error measures. The units in which we chose to measure errors are likely to vary, depending on both the type of variable and the purpose of the error analysis. For data like GNP, consumer expenditures, and investment expenditures, which have strong trend movements, it may be useful to examine errors in predicted percentage growth, as well as conventional units.[3] For variables like interest rates or unemployment rates, which tend to oscillate about some level, errors almost invariably will be expressed in conventional units. These particular errors for rates ought to be measured in percentage (basis) points.

Finally, while it is possible to examine each forecast for each period, it is desirable to be able to summarize errors to make some judgment about what the average error has been. The summary measures used here include the root mean square error (RMSE), mean absolute error (MAE), and mean error (ME).[4]

The typical Wharton quarterly model forecast has been for a period of eight quarters. More recently this has been extended to twelve quarters. The cutoff point is arbitrary, but clearly one or two quarters ahead do not provide useful horizons for policy planning in either the public or private sectors. A model achieves its greatest usefulness in providing consistent accounting balance 1 year or more into the future. Data are available on eight-quarter forecast horizons in intermediate steps of one quarter each, but for comparative purposes, we may look at shorter horizons of five or six quarters. Many judgmental forecasts tend to be shorter than 2 or 3 years. Much longer forecasts have been attempted for consideration of special planning problems, but near-term forecasting is the focus of our present attention.

It is always easier to forecast the economy in an extended cyclical phase of steady growth or decay—the upswing and the downswing. Errors are greater and the challenge is more severe at the turning points. It is of great importance to be prepared for a change of direction in economic movement. Accordingly, we shall look at some turning-point episodes.

The first set of figures is taken from a series of studies by Stephen McNees, who has become a semiofficial referee of economic forecasts. From an objective position at the Federal Reserve Bank of Boston, he collects many kinds of economic forecasts and analyzes their error properties. An interesting comparison is provided by his findings for errors in the judgmental forecasts reported by the American Statistical Association to the National Bureau of Economic Research (ASA/NBER). These are not strictly judgmental because many of those reporting use econometric models or some other formal quantitative method. However, they are often used as a standard by which to judge econometric models. The medians of the ASA/NBER forecasts are used for comparison with model forecasts. In this instance, we shall stack the Wharton model forecasts against the judgmental set.

It should be clear from the discussion in chapter 4 that judgment goes into the Wharton forecasts too. The procedures for specifying exogenous variables and model adjustment, forecast meeting discussions, and forecast revision affect the model's results. It is also true that the results of econometric forecasts go into the calculation of judgmental forecasts. It is a case of comparing a judgmental (partially econometric) forecast with an econometric (partially judgmental) forecast.

Among many possibilities for measuring forecast accuracy, we shall choose mean absolute error of growth rate. We must be careful to express it as a percentage of some significantly nonzero magnitude. The variables that can be at or near zero are residual or difference variables, such as inventory change, net

Table 5-2
Error Analysis, Wharton Forecasts, 1970.3 to 1975.2, Mean Absolute Error

	Forecast Horizon (Quarters)					
	1	2	3	4	5	6
Real GNP (%)	2.2	2.1	2.2	2.1	2.2	2.4
GNP deflator (%)	1.1	1.6	1.8	2.1	2.3	2.6
Unemployment rate (percentage points)	0.2	0.3	0.3	0.3	0.3	0.4
Consumer expenditures, durables (%)	9.0	9.1	7.8	6.3	5.8	5.5
Consumer expenditures, nondurables, services (%)	1.3	1.3	1.3	1.4	1.4	1.5
Business fixed investment (%)	8.0	6.1	4.6	3.8	3.6	3.4
Residential investment (%)	13.4	13.7	12.1	12.0	11.5	11.6

foreign balance, savings, profit, and unemployment. The last mentioned is typically expressed as a percentage of labor force, while the others are generally expressed as ratios to GNP. We compute changes in these ratios and not percentage changes.

The summation of replications is over forecasts of a given horizon—all one-quarter-ahead forecasts, all two-quarter-ahead forecasts, and so on. The forecast errors in table 5-2 are evaluated over the period 1970.3 to 1975.2, a turbulent economic episode in the entire world, spanning the Smithsonian agreement on exchange rates, President Nixon's New Economic Policy, the Watergate era, the oil embargo, and many other notable events.

When the errors are expressed in change form—as error in rates of growth or change in percent unemployed—there is little tendency of the errors to grow with length of the forecast horizon. If the errors were expressed as dollars of real GNP (in absolute value), they would grow fairly rapidly, for example:

	Forecast Horizon (Quarters)					
	1	2	3	4	5	6
Real GNP ($ billion)	4.3	8.3	13.3	17.5	22.5	28.8

The average absolute error grows from $4.3 billion in one quarter to $28.8 billion in six quarters, but in terms of growth rates, it stays just above 2%. The more volatile elements of GNP—expenditures on durables, business fixed investment, and residential investment—have much larger percentage errors. Even though the errors seem to be large for a series like expenditures on residential construction, the Wharton model values of MAE are lower than those of most comparable forecasting performances by others over this period.

All the numbers being considered in table 5-2 are reduced in size and expressed as annual percentage rates of growth, but the errors are reasonably small, often a fraction of a percent, 1%, or 2%, depending on the variable being considered. It is our opinion that effective economic policy and business planning can be made with error bands of this size

In a previous chapter we consider the feedback to econometric modelers from general professional criticism, by means of error tabulations from mid-quarter forecasts, that is, those made after the regular forecast meeting with users of the Wharton model. In this chapter, we extend this comparison to additional variables. In more than one-half the cases, the entry in table 5-3 is lower than the corresponding entry in table 5-2 (twenty-three cases of a possible forty-two). The results are equal in six cases. It appears, therefore, that the meeting leads to improvement. This is not unequivocal in the shortest-length forecasts, however, because there is a 1-month extra accumulation of ability to observe the economy. For the two key variables we noted earlier—the real

Table 5-3

Error Analysis, Postmeeting Wharton Forecasts, 1970.3 to 1975.2, Mean
Absolute Error

	Forecast Horizon (Quarters)					
	1	2	3	4	5	6
Real GNP (%)	1.7	1.7	1.9	1.9	2.0	2.1
GNP deflator (%)	1.1	1.3	1.7	1.9	2.1	2.4
Unemployment rate (percentage points)	0.1	0.3	0.3	0.3	0.3	0.3
Consumer expenditures, durables (%)	8.9	9.4	8.0	7.0	5.9	5.5
Consumer expenditures, nondurables, services (%)	1.3	1.4	1.4	1.2	1.2	1.3
Business fixed investment (%)	8.5	5.8	4.9	3.8	3.4	2.9
Residential investment (%)	11.5	11.4	11.6	12.8	12.7	12.4

growth rate and the inflation rate—the postmeeting forecast is decidedly better than the premeeting forecast. In consumption and investment the results are more mixed.

Another interesting comparison is between a model and a "judgmental" forecast, tabulated from returns of the participants in the survey conducted by the American Statistical Association and reported to the National Bureau of Economic Research.

The ASA/NBER forecasts are not available for a wide range of variables, numbering into the hundreds or possibly thousands, as is the case with formal models, and this is one of the deficiencies of the judgmental method, especially if presented on a consensus or average basis. In the case of the two central variables, however—the growth rates and the inflation rates—the Wharton model consistently outperforms the judgmental forecasts. This is shown clearly in table 5-4. These results have stood up well when the forecast period is updated.[5]

With one exception, the Wharton model results are more accurate. The comparison is restricted to a five-quarter horizon, because this is as far ahead as the ASA/NBER survey goes. It should be noted, too, that the ASA/NBER results almost consistently have a later release date than the Wharton model results (premeeting) reported here. The postmeeting results would be even more favorable for the Wharton model.

When the analysis is extended to other variables, the findings are mixed. They are about the same for the unemployment rate and profit levels, but the ASA/NBER results are better for inventory investment and expenditures on consumer durables. McNees concludes: "Forecasts not based on formal econometric models appeared to be generally as accurate or more accurate than econometrically based forecast." On the basis of the results in table 5-4, we would dispute the validity of that conclusion.

Table 5-4
Error Analysis, Comparison of Wharton Model and ASA Forecasts, 1970.3 to 1975.2, Mean Absolute Error

	Forecast Horizon (Quarters)				
	1	2	3	4	5
Real GNP, (%) ASA	2.1	2.2	2.3	2.5	2.4
Wharton model	2.2	2.1	2.2	2.1	2.2
GNP deflator, (%) ASA	1.8	2.0	2.0	2.3	2.5
Wharton model	1.1	1.6	1.8	2.1	2.3

McNees used another comparison in reaching his conclusion, namely, a comparison with the results of the General Electric Company forecast using an "informal" model combined with a great deal of judgment. On the same two key variables, the Wharton "midquarter" forecasts outperformed the GE late-quarter forecasts most of the time, but not quite as frequently as in the case of the ASA/NBER comparison. For other variables, the results are mixed in the comparison with GE forecasts. The findings are not altered in the updated evaluation.

It is not surprising to find that forecasts by any method fared relatively badly in the turbulent years since 1971. Turning points and change are more difficult to forecast than steady growth or decline. When the economy fell precipitously, the predicted changes were uniformly too high, and when the inflation rate climbed the most, the predicted changes were uniformly too low. As a general rule, economists tend to underestimate change. The period of the oil embargo and the 1974 recession was a severe test for all forecasting techniques.

The National Income and Product Accounts (NIPA) underwent a benchmark revision as of 1976 which included conceptual, statistical, and base-period changes which make comparison of forecasts made before the first quarter of 1976 with forecasts made after that period difficult. The closest comparisons for a variable like GNP will hold for predicted percentage change, which should be little affected by the base-period change. Table 5-5 presents the errors of all Wharton postmeeting GNP forecasts made since 1975 in percentage terms. The lefthand column of the table contains the last available actual percentage change for GNP.[6] A recent report on the growth in constant-dollar GNP from the second quarter of 1978 to the third quarter of 1978 is 0.64. The error in the forecast growth for that period can be read across the line moving back in time. The forecast percentage change for 1978 third quarter from second quarter levels made in the third quarter had an error of 0.17. This is calculated as predicted minus actual, so the forecast growth was 0.81 (= 0.64 + 0.17). The forecast error from the forecast for that period made in the second quarter was 0.49,

Table 5-5

Gross National Product (Constant Dollars) Solution, Postmeeting Forecast Errors, Predicted Percentage Change

Last Available Actual		Forecast Horizon (Quarter)							
		1	2	3	4	5	6	7	8
1976.1	2.25	-0.65							
1976.2	1.00	0.34	0.13						
1976.3	0.67	0.60	0.39	0.81					
1976.4	0.59	0.36	0.98	0.86	0.67				
1977.1	1.77	-0.84	-0.56	-0.53	0.46	-0.66			
1977.2	1.44	0.22	0.99	-0.17	-0.29	-0.19	-0.42		
1977.3	1.39	-0.03	0.43	0.35	-0.40	-0.36	-0.38	-0.55	
1977.4	0.79	0.45	0.33	0.71	0.77	0.68	0.26	0.50	-0.11
1978.1	-0.02	0.90	0.93	0.88	1.28	1.48	1.25	0.77	0.72
1978.2	2.10	0.12	-0.75	-1.11	-1.14	-0.80	-0.75	-0.76	-1.28
1978.3	0.64	0.17	0.49	0.34	0.57	0.38	0.43	0.31	0.54
RMSE		0.51	0.66	0.70	0.77	0.76	0.67	0.60	0.79
MAE		0.42	0.60	0.64	0.70	0.65	0.58	0.58	0.66
ME		0.15	0.34	0.24	0.13	0.08	0.07	0.05	-0.03

and so on. It follows that the errors from any outlook made at a point in time can be read down a diagonal. The quarterly growth rates in the forecast made in 1976.2, for example, had errors of 0.34 for the second quarter, 0.39 for 1976.3, followed by errors of 0.86, 0.46, -0.19, -0.38, 0.50, and 0.72. The root mean square error, mean absolute error, and mean error for one-quarter-ahead, two-quarter-ahead, and so on up to eight-quarter-ahead forecasts appear at the bottom of the table. The forecast record over this period can be compared with the earlier period by multiplying the MAE by 4 and comparing it to the real GNP error measures in table 5-3. With the exception of the one-quarter-ahead forecast, which is only marginally better, this measure of forecast error indicates that forecast-error experience during the expansion period was not substantially better and perhaps somewhat worse than for the period 1970.3 to 1975.2 with respect to real growth. A similar comparison with table 5-6 indicates that the opposite conclusion holds for the implicit deflator. Table 5-7 also indicates some general improvement in projections for the unemployment rate.

The general conclusion to be drawn from these detailed tables is that the Wharton forecasting group has not done appreciably better or worse at forecasting major economic magnitudes during the postrecession period than it did during the 1970-1975 period.

In evaluating the forecast we might also note that there is a general tendency during this latter period to overestimate real growth (the ME is greater

Table 5-6
Implicit Deflator, Gross National Product Solution, Postmeeting Forecast
Errors, Predicted Percentage Change

Last Available Actual		Forecast Horizon (Quarter)							
		1	2	3	4	5	6	7	8
1976.1	0.97	0.35							
1976.2	1.16	0.22	0.52						
1976.3	1.11	0.32	0.33	0.40					
1976.4	1.41	0.08	0.23	0.16	0.15				
1977.1	1.46	0.23	-0.14	0.15	0.08	0.07			
1977.2	1.87	-0.21	-0.14	-0.35	-0.36	-0.21	-0.44		
1977.3	1.26	-0.12	0.24	0.30	-0.10	0.23	0.38	0.09	
1977.4	1.35	0.06	0.38	0.19	0.18	0.05	0.25	0.47	0.25
1978.1	1.76	-0.21	-0.23	-0.18	-0.17	-0.52	-0.58	-0.45	-0.18
1978.2	2.64	-0.42	-1.17	-1.35	-1.25	-1.14	-1.14	-1.33	-1.21
1978.3	1.68	0.08	0.16	-0.13	-0.43	-0.31	-0.07	0.06	0.33
RMSE		0.24	0.46	0.51	0.50	0.50	0.58	0.67	0.65
MAE		0.21	0.35	0.36	0.34	0.36	0.48	0.48	0.49
ME		0.04	-0.01	-0.09	-0.21	-0.26	-0.27	-0.24	-0.37

Table 5-7
Unemployment Rate, Civilian Labor Force Solution, Postmeeting Forecast
Errors, Predicted Percentage Change

Last Available Actual		Forecast Horizon (Quarter)							
		1	2	3	4	5	6	7	8
1976.1	-0.6	0.1							
1976.2	-0.2	0.0	0.2						
1976.3	0.2	-0.2	-0.5	-0.4					
1976.4	0.0	0.0	-0.4	-0.3	-0.2				
1977.1	-0.3	0.3	0.1	0.0	0.0	0.1			
1977.2	-0.4	0.0	-0.1	0.1	0.1	0.2	0.3		
1977.3	-0.2	0.0	-0.1	-0.3	0.0	0.0	0.0	0.1	
1977.4	-0.3	0.2	0.2	-0.1	-0.1	0.0	0.1	0.1	0.2
1978.1	-0.4	0.2	0.5	0.4	0.2	0.1	0.2	0.4	0.3
1978.2	-0.3	0.0	0.2	0.2	0.2	0.1	0.1	0.1	0.3
1978.3	0.1	0.0	-0.2	-0.1	-0.3	-0.1	-0.2	-0.1	-0.3
RMSE		0.14	0.28	0.23	0.15	0.11	0.17	0.19	0.27
MAE		0.10	0.24	0.20	0.13	0.09	0.15	0.15	0.27
ME		0.06	-0.00	-0.04	-0.00	-0.05	-0.08	-0.10	-0.13

than zero for every period except the eighth quarter) and to underestimate the inflation rate (the ME is less than zero for every quarter except the first).

Prospects

What is the outlook for econometric forecasting? Can we expect a dramatic or even a slow decline in forecast errors either at the macroeconomic or more detailed level of the economy? What are the fruitful lines of research to improve the "scientific" aspects of forecasting and reduce the "artistry" required of the forecaster who uses an econometric model?

There are two major lines of research that promise hope of continued evolution of forecasting accuracy and at the same time reduced reliance on intuition and judgment for forecasting. These research areas are in the model structure and in forecasting methodology

As the brief survey in chapters 2 and 3 indicated, there are many shortcomings of the current Wharton model and all other macromodels with regard to specification, estimation techniques, and data resources. Macroeconomic theory only recently has taken the first faltering steps at constructing a choice theoretic structure built on consistent behavior of microeconomic units and dealing with the implications of aggregate descriptions of these data. Few of the large models have been subjected to estimation with techniques appropriate to their simultaneous specification. The few studies done in this area have largely been based on small models that have been grossly misspecified. Data resources are constantly being amplified and updated, particularly with additional data on stocks, more detail on final demand and output, and more frequent reporting and updating.

It is unlikely that improvements expected in any of these areas will revolutionize our understanding of the economy or our ability to explain or anticipate its behavior. But as improvements accumulate in each of these areas, the models are likely to become better approximations of aggregate behavior; the residual component which remains incapable of explanation should shrink; the structure should become more stable; and even when altered, it should become more susceptible to explanation for the cause of the change.

All these developments relate to improvements in the forecasting tool. Research in all these areas goes on quite independent of the econometric model projects and adds to the store of material to be drawn on for model construction. The other research area has drawn much less attention and resources, but may in the short run offer as much or more in rewards to forecasting accuracy. This involves research into the appropriate and efficient manner of using an econometric model for forecasting. We have outlined an approach to forecasting that has evolved over more than 15 years of forecasting the U.S. economy. It is an approach that appears to produce forecasts for major aggregates as accurate or more accurate than any other. It is not the approach we expect to be using in 10 years, or even 5. As models become ever larger and more disaggregated, it becomes more difficult to bring refined human judgment to bear on each relationship that is consistent across the model structure. Means must be developed for relying more heavily on mechanical analysis of errors and production of adjustments where necessary. To the extent that residuals are not white noise, it should be possible to characterize them by some stochastic process that could be used for projecting residuals in the forecast period where data are available at a finer level of disaggregation (monthly for a quarterly model, quarterly for an annual model) of either the same or related variables. We may be able to relate the stochastic process systematically to recent period errors and use it to assist in getting the model on track. Initial investigations in these directions at Wharton and elsewhere are promising.

Will we ever be able to produce forecasts on a purely mechanical basis? One hesitates to say no. *Ever* encompasses a long time. Thirty years ago the prospect of achieving the accuracy and versatility of the current generation of models seemed impossible. We continue to reduce systematic error and endogenize variables subject to control by economic agents Who knows where the computer giants of the next century will stand?

Notes

1. P.A. Samuelson, "The Art and Science of Macromodels over 50 Years," *The Brookings Model: Perspective and Recent Developments.*

2. The discussion of these issues is based on S.K. McNees "An Evaluation of Economic Forecasts," *New England Economic Review,* November/December 1975. Additional issues and more detailed comments can be found there.

3. This is likely to be particularly important when errors are compared over a long time span, or when the relevant magnitudes are growing rapidly.

4. Letting A^f_{t+i} and A_{t+i} represent forecast and actual values for period $t + i$, these are defined as

$$ \text{RMSE} = \sqrt{\frac{\sum_{i=1}^{n}(A^f_{t+i} - A_{t+i})^2}{n}} $$

$$ \text{MAE} = \sum_{i=1}^{n} A^f_{t+i} - A_{t+i}/n $$

$$ME = \sum_{i=1}^{n} (A^f_{t+i} - A_{t+i})/n$$

where A's can be measured in either conventional units or percentage changes

5. S.K. McNees, "An Evaluation of Economic Forecasts: Extension and Update," *New England Economic Review,* September/October 1976, pp. 30–44.

6. The table was produced January 30, 1979.

Index

Index

Adjustment. *See* Model adjustment

Aggregation level, in model specification, 50–56

Agriculture, farm price forecast in, 123

American Statistical Association/National Bureau of Economic Research (ASA/NBER) forecasts, *vs* Wharton model, 140, 142

Annual forecasts, 78–79

Automobile sales equation; adjustment of, 93; consistency evaluation for, 98

Autoregressive-moving-average equation, 6

Average absolute percentage error (AAPE), 66

Behavioral relationships; defined, 17; in macroeconomic models, 18

Bias, in parameter estimates, 81

Box-Jenkins relation, 6

Chart reading, in time-series analysis, 4, 9

Compensation rate, determinants of, 28–31, 30, 37, 42–43

Computers, electronic, in data bank access, 83

Constant term adjustment; defined, 86; examples of, 87–94

Consumer price index, 35–36

Consumption expenditure; behavioral relationships in, 17–18; equation adjustment for, 88t, 90–92; final demand determinants of, 21, 22; and investment expenditure, 14; misspecification of, 22–23; sample survey analysis of, 7

Consumption expenditure and income; aggregation relationship in, 51–52; IS-LM curve of, 7–8

Currency in circulation, equation adjustment for, 87–90, 88

Cyclical indicators, 3, 5

Data, input/output, 24

Data bank; computer access to, 83; incomplete estimation of values for, 75–77; preparation of, 75; revision of, 81–82; update procedure for, 82, 83, 100; verification of, 77–78

Data revision, error calculation and, 138–139

Data sources, 14, 15t; National Income and Product Accounts (NIPA), 11–12; release schedules of, 75–76

Disaggregation; in distributed-lay relationships, 52–54; and forecast error, 54, 73–74; gains and losses from, 55, 56; in model specification, 52

Distributed-lag relationships, estimation of, 52–54

Dynamic multipliers, calculation of, 66–67, 69

Dynamic simulation, 64–65

Economic forecasting. *See* Forecast

Economic indicators, in forecast table, 126–127

Economic models. *See* Models, econometric

Economy, growth rate projections for; U.S., 112–113, 114–115; world, 122–123

Electricity and gas consumption, model for; effects of weather on, 22–23; relative price and income in, 21, 22; total structure in, 23

Employee hours, labor requirements relationship for, 25–28, 27, 42

Employment; labor requirements re-

151

About the Authors

Lawrence R. Klein, Benjamin Franklin Professor of Economics and Finance of the University of Pennsylvania, is chairman of the board of trustees of Wharton Econometric Forecasting Associates, Inc., and principal investigator of Project LINK, an academically oriented research project linking econometric models of various national and regional economies. He is past president of the American Economic Association, Econometric Society, and Eastern Economic Association. He serves as consultant to various private corporations and national and international agencies. He is the author of many books and research papers, as well as an active member of several scientific or scholarly societies.

Richard M. Young is director of the SRI/WEFA World Economic Program at Wharton Econometric Forecasting Associates and an adjunct associate professor at the University of Pennsylvania. He was director of the Wharton U.S. Quarterly Model Project for three years before assuming his present position. He has been associated with econometric model construction and forecasting for the past fifteen years. During this period, he has been an advisor and consultant to numerous government agencies and private-sector enterprises as well as a contributor to professional journals.